BPMN QUICK AND EASY
WITH METHOD & STYLE

Bruce Silver

CODY-CASSIDY PRESS

BPMN Quick and Easy, with Method & Style

By Bruce Silver
ISBN 978-0-9823681-6-9

Published by Cody-Cassidy Press, Altadena, CA 91001 USA
Contact
        info@cody-cassidy.com
        +1 (831) 685-8803

Library of Congress Subject Headings
Workflow -- Management.
Process control -- Data processing -- Management.
Business -- Data processing -- Management.
Management information systems.
Reengineering (Management)
Information resources management.
Agile software development.

Cover design by Leyba Associates

Contents

In the six years since its publication, *BPMN Method and Style 2nd Edition*[1] has become the standard reference for process modelers using the Business Process Model and Notation (BPMN) standard. But over those six years, having delivered BPMN Method and Style training to over 4000 students, I've learned a lot about which parts of the standard are useful and which are best ignored. Where the previous book sought to explain everything in the BPMN spec – with Method and Style layered on top – *BPMN Quick and Easy* seeks to streamline, presenting just those things process modelers need to know. Someone once said, "I would have made it shorter if I had more time." I've had six years now, so it's shorter.

While other business process standards have come and gone – remember BPEL, anyone? – and related ones, like CMMN and DMN, have yet to reach mass adoption, BPMN has become pervasive and remains in wide use today, a good fifteen years after it was originally conceived. That is quite an achievement. And the fact that its primary audience is business users, given their notorious resistance to standards of any sort, is equally impressive.

The main purpose of BPMN is to *communicate* process logic visually, through diagrams that can be shared and discussedcollaboratively, in real time. But that was not the main objective of the BPMN 2.0 task force in the Object Management Group (OMG) back in 2009 when they drafted the spec. Their concern then was unifying the diagramming notation of BPMN 1.2 – already in wide use by process modelers – with precise execution semantics, creating a visual programming language for process automation that could be shared by business and IT. And it's fair to say they succeeded in that, as process automation engines not based on BPMN have fallen by the wayside.[2]

But only a small fraction of BPMN models are used for process automation. Most process modelers don't care a whit about that. They are merely trying to document their current-state process, analyze it for improvement, or redesign it to make it better. And so all those execution-related details crammed into the BPMN 2.0 spec are irrelevant to how the standard is actually used.

---

[1] https://www.amazon.com/dp/B06W5J8P2T

[2] The spec is freely available at http://www.omg.org/spec/BPMN/2.0/

For the vast majority of BPMN users, the only thing that counts is what you can see in the diagrams. The *process logic* – how the process starts and ends, the order of its activities, and its interactions with things outside – should be clearly understandable to anyone from the printed diagrams alone, and not just to those who already know how the process works. At the same time, the process logic captured in those diagrams should be precise and complete. BPMN is not for creating sketches to accompany a detailed text-based process description. Who reads those things, anyway? No. The diagrams *are* the process model.

Good BPMN

That describes the goal, but unfortunately most process models being created by project teams fail that objective. They are *Bad BPMN*. They do not faithfully communicate the modeler's intent. They leave important information out. They can be understood only by those who already know how the process works. And thus the team's huge investment in gathering the information that the model seeks to capture – all those stakeholder workshops and interviews – is, to be honest, wasted.

In this book you're going to learn how to create *Good BPMN*, models that fulfill the objective of clear and complete communication of the process logic. This does not require a technical background, but it does require attention to detail and following the rules. Ultimately process modeling is not meant to be a creative exercise but a disciplined one. While creativity is useful for process improvement or redesign, it is not needed for translating the workings of your process from text into diagrams that everyone can understand. And it's this that is the focus of this book.

Good BPMN means process models that are:

1. *Correct*, according to the concepts, semantics, and rules of the BPMN 2.0 spec

2. *Clear*, so that the process logic is evident to anyone from the printed diagrams alone, without reference to model information hidden in non-visual elements or in attached text documents

3. *Complete*, revealing not only the order of process activities but how the process starts, its possible end states, and all its interactions with things outside: other processes, the requester, service providers, etc.

4. *Consistent* in model structure; given the same set of facts about the process logic, all modelers should create more or less the same set of diagrams

Good BPMN, as I have described it, was never a focus of the BPMN 2.0 task force in 2009, and thus the rules of the spec do not attempt to provide it. The spec deals only with item 1 in the list above. Items 2-4 are not addressed. Those require a methodology and additional rules beyond those laid out in the spec. I call mine *Method and Style*. In this book you'll learn not only the vocabulary of BPMN, the meaning of the shapes and symbols as defined in the spec, but Method and Style as well.

Changes from *BPMN Method and Style, 2nd Edition*

BPMN Method and Style, 2nd Edition still remains the authoritative reference on BPMN 2.0. Available in English, German, Japanese, and Spanish, it describes not only all the shapes and symbols but the non-visual elements also captured in the XML serialization. Because it is comprehensive, addressing implementers and developers in addition to process modelers, it possibly implies to a beginning process modeler that BPMN is more complicated than it really is.

When I wrote it in 2011, I had already trained a few hundred students using the Method and Style approach. Today, I have trained over 4000, using a variety of BPMN tools. I've seen what students like and don't like, and I've adapted the training accordingly. If you've read *BPMN Method and Style* or took my training a few years ago, you might notice that my advice today sometimes differs from what I said in the past. That's true. I am continually trying to make the practice of Good BPMN simpler, more "mechanical" and systematic.

For example, the BPMN spec often gives the modeler multiple ways to diagram the same behavior. I used to teach all the ways; now I see it's better to teach just one way, and *BPMN Quick and Easy* does just that. So you won't see things like activities with multiple outgoing sequence flows, conditional sequence flows, or implicit start and end nodes. Not only are they gone from the book and training, but new style rules warn you away from them. The spec also includes shapes and symbols that are useful only on rare occasions and almost never used correctly. So they're gone, too: Signal events, Conditional events, and Link events... most process modelers can live without them.

Some things have been added. With the new Decision Model and Notation (DMN) standard, BPMN's *decision task* – officially called *business rule task* – now has some real utility, so we talk about how to use it to improve the BPMN. *Event subprocesses* and *data stores* now play more prominent roles in my BPMN Method and Style training, and so they do in the new book, as well.

Message events have always been somewhat problematic because in the spec they mean system-to-system communications to and from the process engine, while in non-executable modeling they are used for any one-way communication between a process element and something outside the process. So should the lane of a *Message end event* imply the sender of the message? The spec says no, but for months students berated me about this. BPMN *Quick and Easy* resolves this conflict.

What You'll Learn

In this book, you're going to learn three things:

1. The vocabulary of BPMN, the shapes and symbols, and how to use them correctly. We're going to focus on just those that you really need to know.

2. A methodology for taking process information gathered from stakeholder interviews and workshops, and reorganizing it into Good BPMN. It is impossible to create

Good BPMN live in real time with the stakeholders. It is a post-process, a "refactoring" of the information. The Method is a systematic five-step procedure for doing that.

3. BPMN Style, additional rules beyond those of the spec, intended to make the process logic clearly understood from the printed diagrams alone. Conforming to the style rules is most easily achieved with BPMN tools that include them in the validation, as do Vizi Modeler from itp commerce, Trisotech BPMN Modeler, and Signavio.

BPMN Tools

While simple BPMN diagrams can be drawn by hand, BPMN assumes use of a software tool. The good news is that there are many such tools to choose from, and the meaning of the diagram is the same with any tool. But even though BPMN is a standard, the tools are not all equally good. Some are really drawing tools, not modeling tools. They can produce diagrams containing the standard shapes and connectors, but the tools do not "understand" their meaning. They cannot, for example, validate the model, or save it in the BPMN standard XML interchange format. If you are serious about process modeling, you need to use a tool that can at least validate your model against the rules of the spec and interchange models with other BPMN tools.

Some BPMN tools are intended for process modelers – business analysts, business architects, and ordinary business users – while others are intended for developers creating automated processes. For most readers of this book, those intended for process modelers will be much easier to use. The great thing about BPMN being a standard is that business and technical users don't need to use the same tool. Models can be interchanged between compliant tools without loss of fidelity. The BPMN Model Interchange Working Group (MIWG)[3] provides a set of tests for model interchange and regularly updates its list of compliant tools (Figure 1-1).

The best BPMN tools (in my opinion) include built-in support for Method and Style. There are currently three that I know of:

- Vizi Modeler from itp commerce is an add-in to Microsoft Visio 2010 or later. An earlier version was called Process Modeler for Visio. Vizi Modeler includes wizard-based model generation following the Method and its model validation feature checks both the spec rules and the style rules.

- Trisotech BPMN Modeler is a cloud/browser-based tool. Style rule validation is built into its toolbar, and the tool integrates BPMN with companion DMN and CMMN models.

- Signavio also provides a cloud/browser-based tool, with style rule validation built in.

---

[3] http://www.omgwiki.org/bpmn-miwg/doku.php

Illustrations in this book were created using both Vizi Modeler and Trisotech.

BPMN Tools tested for Model Interchange

Vendor	Tool	BPMN 2.0	Import	Export	Roundtrip	Demo Participation	Last Test
Trisotech	Trisotech BPMN Modeler 5.2.0	○	○ Diff	○ Diff	○ Details	○ 2017, 2016, 2015, 2014, 2013	○ 2017
Boris Zinchenko	BPMN View 1.0.4	○	○ Diff	⊖	⊖ Details	○ 2017	○ 2017
Esteco S.p.a.	BeePMN 1.3	○	○ Diff	○ Diff	○ Details	○ 2017, 2016	○ 2017
BOC Group	ADONIS 6.0	○	○ Diff	○ Diff	○ Details	○ 2017, 2016, 2015, 2014, 2013	◐ 2016
Signavio GmbH	Signavio Process Editor 10.0.0	○	○ Diff	○ Diff	○ Details	○ 2017, 2016, 2015, 2014, 2013	◐ 2016
W4 Software	W4 BPMN+ Composer V.9.4	○	○ Diff	○ Diff	○ Details	○ 2017, 2016, 2015, 2014, 2013	◐ 2016
Camunda	Camunda Modeler 2.7.0	○	○ Diff	○ Diff	○ Details	○ 2017, 2016, 2015, 2014, 2013	◐ 2015
itp-commerce	itp-commerce Process Modeler for MS Visio 6	○	○ Diff	○ Diff	○ Details	○ 2017, 2016, 2015, 2014, 2013	◐ 2015
ModelFoundry Pty. Ltd.	ModelFoundry 1.1.1	○	○ Diff	○ Diff	○ Details	◐ 2016	◐ 2016
Camunda	bpmn.io 0.9.2	○	○ Diff	○ Diff	○ Details	◐ 2016, 2015, 2014	◐ 2015
Trisotech	Trisotech BPMN Visio Add in 5.0.1	○	○ Diff	○ Diff	○ Details	◐ 2016, 2015, 2014, 2013	◐ 2015
MODELIOSOFT / SOFTEAM	Modelio 3.5	○	○ Diff	○ Diff	○ Details	◐ 2016	◐ 2015
Yaoqiang, Inc.	Yaoqiang BPMN Editor 4.0	○	○ Diff	○ Diff	○ Details	◐ 2016, 2015, 2014, 2013	◐ 2015
GenMyModel	GenMyModel 0.47	○	○ Diff	○ Diff	○ Details	◐ 2015	◐ 2015
Sparx	Enterprise Architect 12.0.1207	○	○ Diff	○ Diff	○ Details	◐ 2015	◐ 2015
Alfresco	Activiti Designer 5.14.1	○	○ Diff	○ Diff	⊖ Details	◐ 2014	◐ 2014
IBM	IBM BlueWorks Live April 2014	○	○ Diff	○ Diff	⊖ Details	◐ 2014	◐ 2014
Oracle	Oracle BPM Studio 12.1.3	○	○ Diff	⊖	⊖ Details	◐ 2014	◐ 2014
Camunda	camunda-bpmn.js 8428718423	○	○ Diff	⊖	⊖ Details	◐ 2013	◐ 2014
Software AG	ARIS Architect 10.0.0	○	○ Diff	○ Diff	⊖ Details	⊖ 0	○ 2017

Figure 1-1. BPMN MIWG tests tool support for model interchange

Beyond Book Learning

BPMN is a new language. You can learn to read it well simply by reading this book. Learning to write it, however, generally requires more than book learning. It requires practice, and testing your knowledge.

An inexpensive and easy way to get practice is through bpmnPRO, a gamification-based eLearning app modeled after Duolingo, a popular iOS language app. It involves no tools or lecture. bpmnPRO teaches BPMN Method and Style entirely through quiz questions and puzzles.

Becoming truly proficient in BPMN, however, requires a bit of training, connecting the book learning or lecture material with hands-on experience using a tool. *BPMN Quick and Easy* provides many diagram examples, and I encourage readers to reproduce them using a BPMN tool. Like any skill, you really learn BPMN only by *doing* it, working through the creation of diagrams that faithfully represent some given process scenario. In other words, you need a bit of BPMN *training*.

There is an old joke about sex education vs. sex training that I won't repeat here. But you get the idea. Training involves practice, exercises and discussion of solutions, why certain ways work better than others. I provide BPMN Method and Style training, both live and online, in various formats and using a variety of tools[4]. This book could be used as a reference for that training, or as a textbook in a college course on BPMN, but by itself it is not training.

Structure of the Book

The organization of the book largely follows that of my BPMN Method and Style training.

Chapter 1, *What Is BPMN?*, discusses four key differences between BPMN and traditional swimlane flowcharts, which it outwardly resembles. It also explains the limitations of BPMN, the types of processes it cannot describe, and the aspects of process modeling that are outside its purview. It explains the real meaning of BPMN's most fundamental concepts – *activity* and *process* – and the issues that arise when BPM Architecture and other segments of the BPM domain use those terms much more loosely.

Chapter 2, *BPMN by Example*, builds up an order process bit by bit using elements of the Level 1 working set, mostly shapes carried over from traditional flowcharting. Readers learn the meaning and basic usage of tasks and subprocesses, start and end events, gateways, pools, and lanes, and message flow. At the same time, they learn the basics of Method and Style, including process levels and end states, with label matching between gateways in the parent level and end states in the child level. They learn the three possible ways a process can start, and how that tells you what the process instance represents.

Chapter 3, *The Method*, deals with the real challenge of process modeling: translating the tangle of process details gathered from stakeholder interviews and workshops into properly structured BPMN that communicates the process logic clearly from the printed diagrams alone. The Method is a systematic five-step procedure. It is not done in real time with the stakeholders, but involves carefully reorganizing that information afterwards in top-down fashion.

Chapter 4, *BPMN Style*, explains why the rules of the BPMN spec are inadequate to ensuring Good BPMN and the benefits of formulating Good BPMN practices as additional style rules that can be validated by tools. It then explains the most important style rules, illustrating both violations and correct BPMN style.

Chapter 5, *DMN and Decision Tasks*, discusses why embedding decision logic in process models as a chain of gateways is Bad BPMN, and how integrating BPMN with the new companion standard DMN fixes the problem. The chapter includes a tutorial on DMN basics, and provides a simple procedure for transforming embedded decision logic into a decision task (aka business rule task) invoking a DMN decision, followed by a single gateway.

---

[4] For more information, see methodandstyle.com.

Chapter 6, *Parallel Flow*, explains the concepts and issues of conditionally parallel flow using OR gateways, and use of the proper gateway to merge sequence flows, depending upon whether they are exclusive alternatives, unconditionally parallel, or conditionally parallel.

Chapter 7, *Events*, discusses common usage patterns with the Big 3 event types: Timer, Message, and Error. Readers learn how to model deadline-triggered actions, wait for a message or a timeout, handle cancellation or update of a process in flight, and use error throw-catch patterns. The main focus is on intermediate events, but the chapter also describes the use of event subprocesses.

Chapter 8, *Instance Alignment*, returns to an issue introduced in Chapter 1, the spec's requirement that the instance of every activity in a BPMN process must correspond 1:1 with the process instance. That means, for example, that in a process where the instance is an order, every activity must be performed once per order, not once a day or once a batch of orders. Of course, batching is commonplace in real processes, and this chapter discusses various ways to handle it: loop and multi-instance activities, multi-process structures, and non-interrupting event subprocesses.

Chapter 9, *Becoming Proficient*, discusses how to go beyond "book learning" and become really proficient at Good BPMN. It takes practice, testing your understanding, and hands-on experience with real tools. Training including certification is usually a big help.

Bruce Silver
October 2017

CHAPTER 1

What Is BPMN?

BPMN stands for *Business Process Model and Notation*. For the vast majority of BPMN users, the most important part is the N – the graphical *notation* – a diagramming language for business process flows. The most important thing about it is that it is a *standard,* maintained by the Object Management Group (OMG). That means it is not owned or controlled by a single tool vendor or consultancy. You pay no fee or royalty to use the intellectual property it represents. The meaning of a diagram is not determined by a particular tool or the imagination of the modeler; it's defined in a specification. It means the same thing in any tool.

BPMN is an *expressive* language, able to describe nuances of process behavior compactly in the diagram. At the same time, the meaning is precise enough to describe the technical details that control process execution in an automation engine! Thus BPMN bridges the worlds of business and IT, a common process language that can be shared between them. Today, virtually every process modeling tool supports BPMN in some fashion, even though a few vendors may grumble that their own proprietary notation is better or more business-friendly.

Differences from Swimlane Flowcharts

When BPMN 1.0 was first created, adoption by business users was a primary goal. Accordingly, the notation adopted the outward look of traditional *swimlane flowcharts*. Its boxes and arrows, diamonds and swimlanes were already familiar to business people. Undoubtedly that familiarity accounts for much of BPMN's popularity with business users today. But the other side of the coin is that familiarity has bred misuse. Modelers think they already know the language, and this leads to mistakes. Although the notation is outwardly similar to traditional flowcharting, BPMN's importance today derives from all the ways in which it is *different*.

One difference, already mentioned, is that modelers may not make up their own meaning for the shapes and symbols. BPMN is based on a specification, defining a formal *metamodel* with specific attributes and precise semantics for each shape and symbol. It has *rules* that govern the use of each one, what may connect to what. Thus you can *validate* a BPMN model, and any BPMN tool worth using can do that in one click of the mouse.

A second key difference from traditional flowcharts is that BPMN is inherently hierarchical. A single process model is not restricted to one diagram but more often is a hierarchical set of diagrams. The element linking the parent and child levels in the hierarchy is called a subprocess, which is simultaneously a single activity and a process flow from start event to end event. Subprocesses allow process details to be condensed visually so that the entire end-to-end process fits on a single page, with all details retained and visualized by drilling down into child-level diagrams. BPM as a management discipline asks you to understand, measure, and manage the business from the perspective of end-to-end cross-functional processes, and BPMN's hierarchical structure lets you do that.

A third important difference is BPMN allows you to *visualize interactions between the process and things outside*: the Customer, service providers, and other internal processes. In addition to sequence flows, the solid arrows representing activity flow inside the process, BPMN diagrams include message flows, dashed arrows representing those interactions, along with interactions via shared data. This places the process being modeled more clearly in the broader enterprise context.

Fourth, unlike flowcharts, BPMN allows you to *visualize in the diagrams event-triggered behavior*. An event is "something that happens" while the process is underway: The customer cancels an order in process, an expected response does not arrive in time, or a system is down. These things happen all the time. BPMN lets you describe in the diagram *what should happen* when those exceptions occur.

Thus, using BPMN correctly and effectively requires learning the parts of it that are missing in traditional flowcharts and thus may be *unfamiliar*. It's not hard, and that is what this book is about.

The Limits of BPMN

It is important to recognize that not all business processes can be described by BPMN, and for even those that can, BPMN does not describe everything you need.

BPMN cannot describe, for example, *management processes*. Their names typically start with verbs like Manage, Monitor, or Maintain. Your company's BPM architecture is probably filled with processes like this. But BPMN only describes *processes performed repeatedly on instances*, each instance of the process having a definite start and end. Fulfilling an order is a process performed repeatedly on instances, once per order. But management processes are not performed repeatedly on instances. They are performed, so to speak, continuously. BPMN has no good way to show the sequence of activities that they include. In BPMN models, management processes are best represented abstractly as *black-box pools* interacting with the BPMN process via message flows and shared data.

BPMN also cannot describe *unstructured processes*, sometimes called *case management*. A BPMN process model, in theory, represents every sequence of activities leading from some initial state – the start event – to any possible end state. In other words, the process logic from start to end must be defined in advance. So you cannot have the situation where, at some activity in the middle of the process it is determined that some new unanticipated activity is required. Of course, those situations occur all the time in real life. It's just that BPMN is not well suited to model them. We now have a sister standard, *Case Management Model and Notation* (CMMN), to handle those.

Fortunately, the reason we are still talking about BPMN today is that a great number of business processes do meet its prerequisites: They are performed repeatedly on instances, and all instances follow some process model path defined in advance. But even for those, BPMN does not describe everything a modeler might be asked to document.

BPMN only describes the *process logic* – how the process starts and ends, the order of its activities, and its interactions with external entities. That leaves out a lot:

- Task logic, the internal details of individual activities, such as the task user interface or subtasks.

- Process data

- Organizational structure and roles

- Decision logic and business rules

- Systems and services involved in the process

- Process metrics and KPIs

- Simulation parameters, such as the mean time to complete an activity

Now you might want to tell me that your BPMN tool lets you model many, possibly all, of these things. But they are outside the scope of the BPMN standard. It is safe to say that the way your tool models them is proprietary to that tool. The thing that is common to all tools is the process logic, which is defined by BPMN.

How Does A Model Mean?

A process model is more than a drawing. Its purpose is to convey meaning, specifically the logic of the activity flow from process start to end. From the diagram alone, the process logic should be clear and understandable to a business person but with the semantic precision required by a developer. By *process logic*, we mean a description of all the paths from the initial state of a process instance to any of its possible end states.

The BPMN specification describes each shape and symbol in isolation, defining the meaning of the element. But, as John Ciardi wrote in his classic, *How Does a Poem Mean?*, "the language of experience is not the language of classification." Effectively communicating the process logic requires understanding *how the elements work together*, not just as isolated words but as sentences, paragraphs, a complete story. That requires attention to the overall structure of the model, following a consistent set of conventions, what I call Method and Style. If you do that correctly, the most important features of the process become obvious at a glance: how the process starts, what the instance represents, the process's possible end states, and its interactions with external entities.

We need to convey as much meaning as possible from the diagram by itself, as it would appear in printed form, where all we have are shapes, symbols, and labels. *Labels* are very important. A key piece of the Method and Style approach deals with element labeling, ensuring the process logic is not only clear on each page but traceable from top to bottom in a hierarchical set of diagrams.

We don't want to guess the modeler's intent. It should be obvious from the diagram alone. That's what we mean by Good BPMN. Fortunately, it is a readily learnable skill.

BPMN's Hidden Conceptual Framework

An important source of Bad BPMN has nothing to do with violating Method and Style. I'm talking about models that are *structurally invalid* according to the BPMN metamodel. The reason this occurs so often is that the spec fails to explain the real meaning of BPMN's most fundamental concepts, *activity* and *process*. That failure creates problems not only for beginning process modelers but for experienced business process architects.

Activity and Process

Let's start with *activity*. An activity in BPMN is an *action*, a unit of work performed. It is the only BPMN element that has a *performer*. But the meaning of a BPMN activity is more specific than that. A BPMN activity is an action that is performed *repeatedly on instances*. Each *instance* of the activity represents the same action (more or less) on a different piece of work. The modeler needs to have clarity on the *meaning* of the activity instance, such as an order, a service request, or a monthly review.

Each instance of the activity is a discrete action with a *well-defined start and end*. Once it has ended, it's over, complete. It's not just lying dormant, ready to suddenly reawaken and do a bit more if something happens. It is possible for a process to loop back and repeat an activity, but that would be a separate instance of the activity.

Similarly, a BPMN *process* is also performed repeatedly on instances. A process defines the sequence of activities leading from an initial state of the process instance to some end state. The start of a process is normally marked by a triggering event, such as receipt of a request. The *process model* is a map of *all* the possible paths – all sequences of activities – from that initiating event to any defined end state, success or exception.

Now here is what's critically important about this, and I haven't seen it discussed in other books about BPMN: *In a BPMN process, the instance of each of its activities must correspond 1:1 with the process instance.* For example, if the instance of a process is an order – meaning the process is performed once per order – every activity in that process must be once per order as well. Activities that are performed once a day or once a truckload of orders cannot be part of that process. They must be in some other BPMN process with a corresponding instance, once a day or a truckload batch. This is not Method and Style; this is a consequence of how the BPMN metamodel defines activity and process.

But too frequently we see process models that violate this constraint, even from experienced modelers. These models are structurally invalid, absolutely incorrect. They could not be executed on a BPMN process engine. And this is an error that validation in the tool cannot detect.

This is why modelers need to understand exactly what the instance of their process represents. Fortunately, Method and Style tells you that. We'll see how shortly.

Conflict with BPM Architecture

This problem is doubly unfortunate because BPMN's definition of activity and process is at odds with their definition in other parts of the BPM domain, such as BPM architecture. For example, BPM architecture describes various *business process frameworks*, such as SCOR, ITIL, or eTOM, that enumerate the major processes and activities for a particular industry for the purpose of cross-company benchmarking[5]. For example, APQC publishes a Process Classification Framework (PCF)[6], a hierarchy consisting of Categories, Process Groups, Processes, and Activities for various industries. But few of the processes and activities listed in the PCF conform to BPMN's notion of process and activity. Most are of the *Manage X* variety, representing *business functions* or *capabilities* rather than actions performed repeatedly on instances.

For example, below is a snippet of the PCF for the process called *Process Expense Reimbursements*[7]. In the PCF, the three-digit headings are processes and four-digit headings are activities, presumably activities in that process.

> 8.6.2 Process expense reimbursements (10757)
> > 8.6.2.1 Establish and communicate expense reimbursement policies and approval limits (10880)
> > 8.6.2.2 Capture and report relevant tax data (10881)
> > 8.6.2.3 Approve reimbursements and advances (10882)
> > 8.6.2.4 Process reimbursements and advances (10883)
> > 8.6.2.5 Manage personal accounts (10884)

This particular process is performed repeatedly on instances – once per expernse report – so it does represent a BPMN process. But the activities listed would not all be BPMN activities in

---

[5] See, for example, Paul Harmon, <u>Business Process Change</u>, 2nd edition, Morgan Kauffman, 2007.

[6] http://www.apqc.org/process-classification-framework

[7] http://www.apqc.org/knowledge-base/download/31928/a%3A1%3A%7Bi%3A1%3Bs%3A1%3A%222%22%3B%7D/PCF_Cross%20Industry_v5%202%200.pdf?destination=node/31928

this process. If you tried to wire those activities together in BPMN to define the process, you would fail. Let's see why.

1. Establish the reimbursement policies. That is done once a year, or every few years, certainly not with each expense report. So this is a BPMN activity, but not in this process.

2. Capture and report tax data. Capturing the tax data is once per expense report, but "reporting" it is questionable. If you mean reporting to the tax authority, that is quarterly or annually. If you mean reporting to some internal system, that could be correct, but it is really part of "capturing." Naming of activities should not be ambiguous like this.

3. Approving the reimbursement. This is OK, once per expense report.

4. "Processing" the reimbursement. I assume this means issuing payment, in which case it's OK, but it is not good practice to name a process and an activity within it the same thing... especially when the verb used, "process", has a different meaning in each place.

5. Manage personal accounts. This is not performed repeatedly on instances, so not even a BPMN activity at all. It is a business function or capability.

If APQC cared about aligning its PCF with BPMN, a better activity list for processing employee expense reimbursements might be as follows, where an instance of each activity is a single expense report:

8.6.2 Process expense reimbursements
    8.6.2.1 Review expense report and supporting documentation
    8.6.2.2 Approve reimbursement
    8.6.2.3 Capture tax data
    8.6.2.4 Issue payment

I don't mean to pick on APQC in particular. This problem is pervasive in the literature of business architecture and enterprise BPM. I have come across situations where a BPM architecture team has defined a list of major "activities" that are not discrete actions performed repeatedly on instances with well-defined start and end points, and has then tasked process modelers with wiring them together to describe end-to-end processes. But that is impossible.

OK, enough background. We said "Quick and Easy." So let's get started!

CHAPTER 2

BPMN by Example

A Simple Order Flow

Consider this activity flow for handling an order. The company receives the order, checks the buyer's credit, fulfills the order, and sends an invoice. In simplest terms, that looks like this in BPMN:

Figure 2-1. A simple order flow

The thin circle at the start of the process is called a *start event*. It indicates where the process starts. The icon inside represents the *trigger*. The white envelope trigger means receipt of a message. A *Message start event*, which should be labeled "Receive [message name]", means create a new process instance on receiving the message.

The thick circle at the end is called an *end event*, signifying the process is complete. In Method and Style we label it with the name of the *end state*, Noun-adjective, describing *how* the process ended.

The rounded rectangles are *activities*. An activity represents an *action*, a specific unit of work performed. To reinforce this, activities should have names of the form Verb-object, like *Check credit*, not a *function* (e.g., *Credit Check*) or a *state* (e.g., *Credit OK*).

The solid arrows are called *sequence flows*. When the element at the tail end is complete, the flow moves immediately to the element at the head.

A Process Model

Figure 2-1 is not a process model, however. It simply depicts one path from the initial state *Receive order* to the end state *Order complete*. A *process model* shows all paths to *any possible end state.* And we have a pretty good idea that this is more than shown in Figure 2-1 because we are fulfilling the order on credit, requesting payment only after the goods are shipped.

Before we fulfill the order, we check the Customer's credit. That implies the possibility that in some instances, *Check credit* returns a result that says we don't want to fulfill this particular order; the Customer has Bad credit. In Method and Style we would say that *Check credit* ends in the state *Bad credit* instead of the normal success end state *Credit ok*. In that case we don't want to go to *Fulfill order* but to some other next step instead. We could contact the Customer, get him to pay in advance or some other resolution, but to keep things really simple we'll say if *Check credit* ends in the state *Bad credit*, just end the process.

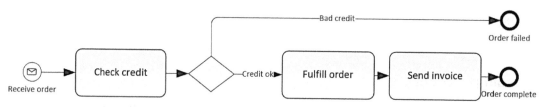

Figure 2-2. Order process with *Bad credit* exception

The diamond shape in Figure 2-2 is called a *gateway*. It represents a branch point in the flow. BPMN provides a number of different gateway types, but this one – the *exclusive data-based gateway* (more commonly called an *XOR gateway*), a diamond with no symbol inside[8] – means take one path or the other based on some data condition.

The BPMN spec technically allows the condition on each outgoing sequence flow, or *gate*, to test any data known to the process at that point. But process modeling tools typically don't define the data elements, so there is a disconnect between the spec and process modeling in practice. Method and Style resolves this problem by adding a constraint: *An XOR gateway always tests the end state of the previous activity.* The gate labels name the end states. So here the gateway asks the question, did *Check credit* end in the state *Credit ok* or *Bad credit*? If *Credit ok*, go on to *Fulfill order*; if *Bad credit*, end the process.

And notice something else: If *Bad credit*, we don't just skip to the end state *Order complete*. The instance of this process, an order, is not complete. It's failed. So we have a second end event labeled Noun-adjective with the end state *Order failed*. BPMN does not require multiple end events like this, but Method and Style says that *each end event in a process or subprocess represents a distinct end state.*

Now it's also possible that *Fulfill order* is unable to complete successfully. The item may be out of stock, and in that case we don't want to send the invoice. Again, to keep this model really simple, we'll say that if *Fulfill order* ends in the state *Item out of stock* we'll end the process in the state *Order failed*. So our process model now looks like Figure 2-3.

---

[8] An X inside the diamond also means the same thing. The spec says just choose one convention – nothing inside or X inside – and stick with it. In this book an XOR gateway has nothing inside.

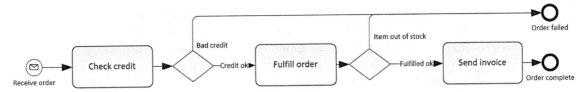

Figure 2-3. Order process with multiple exception paths

Exception end states of an activity don't have to end the process. They can lead to some remedial action and loop back or continue on to wherever you want. Also notice that the diagram now describes three distinct paths from beginning to end. Not all of the model's activities are performed for every instance of the process. If the credit check fails, for example, we do not fulfill the order. If the order items are not in stock, we do not send the invoice. This is common sense, and the process model indicates this explicitly.

Activity Types

BPMN also lets us indicate the *type of activity* through icons and markers (Figure 2-4). There are two basic activity types, tasks and subprocesses. A *task* is atomic, meaning it has no internal subparts described by the model. A *subprocess* is compound; BPMN describes its subparts as a flow from start event to some end state, just like a process.

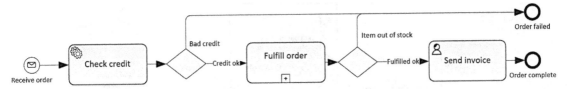

Figure 2-4. Order process in swimlanes

BPMN defines a number of *task types* distinguished by an icon in the top left corner. It is generally useful to distinguish human tasks from automated ones, and these are indicated in the diagram by different *task type icons*. *Send invoice* is a human task, called a *user task* in BPMN. *Check credit* is an automated task, called a *service task* in BPMN. Automated means executed with zero human intervention. If a person pushes a button once and the rest of the task is automated, that is a user task, not a service task.

Fulfill Order is a *subprocess*, one of BPMN's most important concepts. A subprocess is an activity containing subparts that can be expressed as a process flow. In contrast, a *task* is an activity with no defined subparts. A *collapsed subprocess* is rendered as a single activity with a [+] marker. The subprocess details are normally drawn in a separate hyperlinked diagram.

Process Levels

A subprocess is simultaneously an *activity*, a process step that performs work, and a *process*, a flow of activities from a start event to one or more end events. In the model, a single subprocess is usually rendered both *collapsed*, as a single activity shape with the [+] marker, and *expanded* as a process diagram in its own right. The diagram containing the collapsed subprocess has a *parent-to-child relationship* with the diagram containing the subprocess expansion. Thus a single BPMN model is typically a *hierarchy of diagrams,* usually a single top-level diagram and a number of child-level diagrams containing the details of each subprocess. The hierarchy is not limited to two levels. A child-level diagram might itself contain collapsed subprocesses, which are expanded in grandchild-level diagrams.

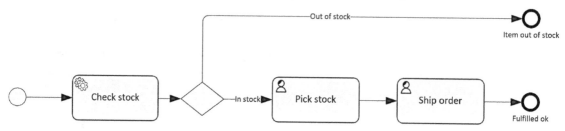

Figure 2-5. Child level of *Fulfill order*

Figure 2-5 illustrates the child level of *Fulfill order.* First the stock is checked automatically. The item could be *In stock,* in which case the flow continues to *Pick stock* and *Ship order* and ends in the child level end state *Fulfilled ok,* or *Out of stock,* in which case the subprocess ends immediately in the end state *Item out of stock.*

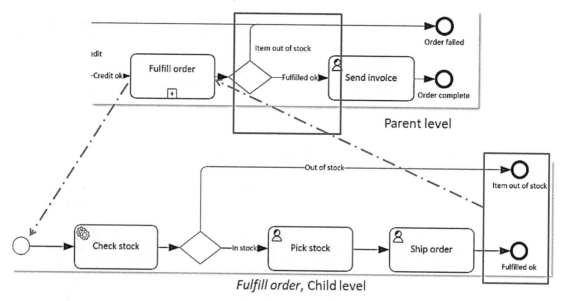

Figure 2-6. Gateway tests child-level end states

Now notice a key feature of Method and Style, illustrated in Figure 2-6. Recall that a gateway tests the end state of the prior activity, with one gate per end state. In a task, the end states are invisible; you can't look inside a task. But you can look inside a subprocess. Its end states are the end events, one end event per end state, indicated by the end event label. So in Method and Style, when a subprocess is followed by a gateway, *the count of gates must match the count of child level end states,* and their names must match as well. Here we have *Fulfilled ok* and *Item out of stock.* This is an example of a *style rule.*

The child level must have an untriggered, or *None,* start event. That's because what starts the subprocess is not an event but the arrival of the sequence flow at the subprocess in the parent level. This is also illustrated in Figure 2-6 by the dash-dot arrows. When the sequence flow arrives in the parent level, the process continues immediately out of the child level start event, and when the child level is complete, the flow continues on the outgoing sequence flow in the parent level. If the child level has multiple end states, the outgoing sequence flow immediately connects to a gateway asking which end state did the instance hit. Each child level end state corresponds to a different gate and next step in the parent level flow.

I should mention that it is possible to draw the child level and parent level in the same diagram, what is called *inline expansion,* using the *expanded subprocess* shape (Figure 2-7). It has the advantage of seeing the parent/child-level label matching in a single diagram, but in our top-down methodology inline expansion is rarely convenient, especially when the diagram contains pools and lanes.

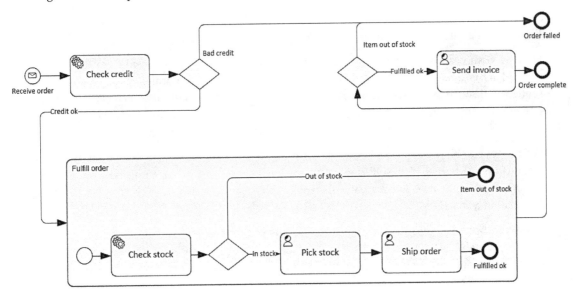

Figure 2-7. Inline expansion

The BPMN spec does not place any significance on whether a sequence flow enters an activity from the left, right, top, or bottom. These are really matters of personal style. I usually try to draw the flow left to right with sequence flows entering activities from the left and exiting from the right, but it depends somewhat on the tool. It takes some rearranging to keep line crossings at a minimum, and sometimes that cannot be avoided. But keeping the diagram as neat and consistently organized as possible is the most important thing. Nothing is more frustrating than looking at a diagram someone else has created and being unsure where exactly the process starts and ends.

Parallel Split and Join

Now let's consider one last detail of our *Fulfill order* subprocess. In order to expedite shipment, we'd like to make the shipping arrangements concurrently with picking the stock, that is, in parallel. We originally considered making these arrangements to be part of *Ship order*, but technically that means we don't do it until after *Pick stock* completes. So we'll modify our model and break *Ship order* into two tasks, *Arrange Shipment* – performed in parallel with *Pick stock* – and *Load truck*.

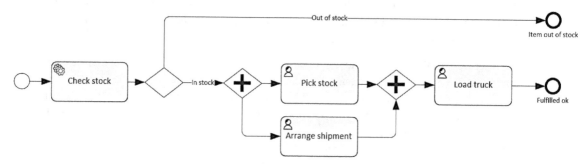

Figure 2-8. Parallel split and join

Figure 2-8 shows how it looks. This uses a gateway with a + symbol inside , in fact two of them. This is a *parallel gateway*, also called an *AND-gateway*. A parallel gateway with one sequence flow in and two or more out is called a *parallel split* or *AND-split*. It means unconditionally split the flow into parallel, i.e., concurrent, segments. Both *Pick Stock* and *Arrange Shipment* are enabled to start at the same time and run concurently.

We cannot combine this parallel gateway with the XOR gateway that precedes it because they mean different things. The XOR gateway is an exclusive decision, meaning take one path or the other. *After* we take the *yes* path, then the AND-split says we do *Pick Stock* and *Arrange Shipment* in parallel.

The second parallel gateway, with multiple sequence flows in and one out, is called an *AND-join* or *parallel join*. It means wait for *all* of the incoming sequence flows to arrive before enabling the outgoing sequence flow. In plain English, it means *Load truck* cannot occur until both *Pick stock* and *Arrange shipment* are complete.

Parallel gateways and their gates should always be unlabeled.

When a process level contains parallel flow and one parallel path reaches an end event, the process level is not yet complete. It is not complete until *all* parallel paths reach an end event. In some cases this requirement can lead to deadlocks, and we'll talk about how to resolve those later on. Usually parallel paths will merge in a join, but not always. They may even lead to separate end events, although this is strongly discouraged because it breaks the Method and Style principle that each end event should represent a distinct end state.

Pools and Lanes

If you've done process modeling before, you're probably asking, *Where are the swimlanes?* We're getting to those now. In the Method, they get added last, for a couple reasons: First, they make the drawing much more complicated and really slow you down. Second, the drawing complexity allows structural errors to creep into the model undetected. I would rather get the structure right up front, and add the pools and lanes – which just indicate who is doing what – at the end.

The spec calls both *pool* and *lane* a type of "swimlane," but this is legacy terminology and in fact misleading. Pools and lanes are completely different things! A *pool* is a rectangular shape that serves as a *container for a process*. The pool shape is optional. Its purpose is to distinguish two different processes interacting via messages and shared data in a single top-level diagram. If you don't have that – which is quite often the case – you may omit the pool shape.

In the BPMN metamodel, a pool represents a "participant" in such a multi-party interaction. Specifically, it represents *the process itself* in its interaction with some outside entity. Consequently *the label of the pool should always be the name of the process.* People often misconstrue the term "participant" to mean the same thing as "performer," the actor or system resource performing a process activity. But this is incorrect; participant and performer are not the same thing.

A *lane* is also an optional rectangular shape. Its purpose is to indicate the performer of the process activities it contains, and is labeled as a role or organizational unit. Some tools require lanes to be enclosed in a pool, but that is a requirement of the tool for drawing purposes. The BPMN spec has no such requirement. Figure 2-9 illustrates our order process with a pool and lanes added.

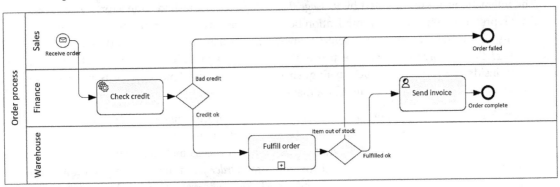

Figure 2-9. Add pool and lanes

Lanes only apply to activities, not gateways or events. I typically put gateways in the same lane as the prior activity, and events wherever they make the diagram look neat. If you use lanes, all activities must be in one lane or another. An activity may not straddle two lanes, and you may not have some activities in a lane and others in no lane at all.

Lanes are defined independently at each process level. It is not uncommon to omit lanes in a top-level diagram, where a subprocess often involves multiple roles and organizational units, but use lanes in child-level diagrams.

Message Flows and Black-Box Pools

Experienced flowcharters new to BPMN often make the Customer a lane inside the process, and start the process with tasks in that lane like *Fill out order form* and *Submit order*. But that is incorrect. Actually, the Customer is *external* to the process, not part of it. Think about an online store like Amazon.com. Have you ever put some item in your Amazon shopping cart but, in the end, decided not to order it after all? Of course you have! Now in that situation, have you created an instance of Amazon's order process? You have not. Amazon's order process starts when they receive the order, even though Amazon itself provides the shopping cart. The order process includes securing payment, retrieving the order items from the warehouse, and delivering them to the Customer.

The Customer in this case is external, not part of the process. This is a fundamental point, and we will discuss it further, but for now just believe me when I say that in most processes the initiator is an *external participant*, not a lane inside the process.

We model an external entity like the Customer as a separate *pool* in our diagram. But unlike the pool that contains the *Order Process*, the Customer pool is empty. It contains no flow elements whatsoever. It's called a *black-box pool.* In the BPMN metamodel, a black-box pool has no associated process. The Customer might not have a BPMN buying process at all, or if he does, its details are invisible to the order fulfillment process. The Customer black-box pool simply represents an external participant interacting with our process.

The interactions are represented by *message flows*, depicted as dashed connectors. A message flow represents a one-way communication between a message node in the process – either an activity or Message event – and some element *outside the process*. This part is critical: A message flow always connects the process to something outside. An email between two actors inside the process – which in English you would call a "message" – is *not* a BPMN message, and cannot be represented by a message flow.

Figure 2-10 shows the Customer interactions with our process using a black-box pool and message flows. Message flows should be labeled with the name of the message, a noun. The *Order* message to the start event is what creates a new process instance. The user task *Send invoice* sends the *Invoice* message. And the end state *Order failed*, here designated a *Message end event* with the black envelope icon, sends the *Failure notice* message. A *Message end event* signifies that the process sends a message when the end event is reached.

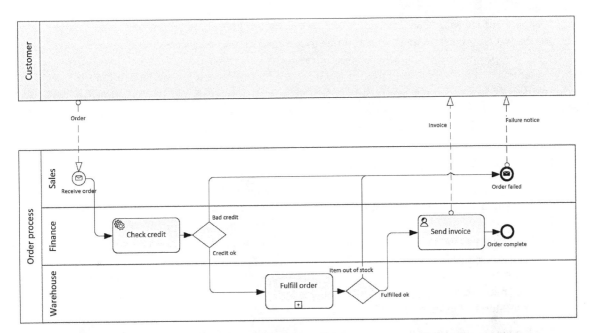

Figure 2-10. Customer interactions with message flows

As we said previously, the idea that the Customer in Figure 2-10 is not part of the process, but external to it, is a surprise to many experienced flowcharters. But actually, this idea goes all the way back to the Rummler-Brache diagrams of the 1980s, the first swimlane diagrams. Geary Rummler was one of the first analysts of business performance from a process perspective and a great influence on the management discipline of BPM. Paul Harmon, editor of BPTrends and a former colleague of Rummler's, recounts[9]:

> An IBM researcher took Rummler's courses and was so impressed with the power of Rummler-Brache diagrams that he created an IBM process methodology called LOVEM. The acronym stood for Line of Vision Enterprise Methodology. The "line", in this case, referred to the swimlane line at the top of a Rummler-Brache diagram that divided the customer from the process and allowed the analyst to see exactly how the process interacted with the customer.

Inherent in analysis of process performance is the interaction of a process with its "customer." In Rummler-Brache and derivatives like LOVEM, the customer was drawn in the top swimlane, and communications across that line represented the customer's perspective on the process. In BPMN, the notation has changed slightly – we show external participants in separate pools – but the concept remains the same.

The same modelers who initially want to make Customer a lane inside the process often insist on inserting activities like *Fill out order form* or *Submit order* inside the Customer pool. That is

---

[9] Paul Harmon, BPTrends Advisor, December 8, 2008,
http://www.bptrends.com/publicationfiles/advisor20081209.pdf

not only unnecessary but incorrect. A pool containing flow elements is, by definition, a *process pool*, not black-box. As such, it has to represent the *complete* process from start to end. So if you put an end event after *Submit order* in the Customer pool, how do you receive the replacement offer, rejection notice, or invoice? You cannot draw those message flows to the boundary of a process pool, only to the boundary of a black-box pool. To draw those message flows you would be forced to draw a complete buyer process for the Customer. But if you are the seller, do you even know the buyer's process? Probably not.

Start Events and the Process Instance

The Message start event in Figure 2-10 is significant in another way. A Message start event indicates that the process *starts upon receipt of an external request*. Here the request takes the form of an order, but a loan application, an insurance claim, or customer service request are all examples of request messages that initiate a process. Message start events should be named *Receive [name of message]*, such as *Receive Order*. Not all processes are triggered by a request message, but most are. A Message start event always signifies a process started by an external request, and the pool – usually black-box – at the tail of the message flow identifies the requester, in this case *Customer*.

But here is the important thing: *The start message identifies the process instance.* In this case, for example, the start message is *Order*, so the process instance is an order. You may recall that BPMN requires that the instance of every activity in a process must correspond 1:1 with the process instance, so it is critical that the modeler understand what the process instance is. Since the majority of processes are started with a message, this clue is very handy: The instance is indicated by the start message.

A Message start event always signifies that the process is started by *external* request. The requester is not necessarily the Customer. It could be, for example, another internal process. Employee-facing processes are a gray area. Is the Employee external or internal to the process? It depends. Sometimes it is better to model the Employee as an external black-box pool, and other times better to make Employee a lane inside the process pool. Here are my guidelines about modeling the requester.

1. The requester is considered *external* – modeled as a black-box pool – if *either* of these conditions is true:

    a. the requester is not part of the organization that provides the process, or

    b. the requester is part of the organization that provides the process but has no regular defined tasks to perform in the process.

2. The requester is considered *internal* to the process if he is part of the organization that performs the process *and* has regular tasks to perform within it. In that case we use an untriggered (None) start event, typically in a lane representing the requester.

Only Three Ways a Process Can Start

Here is another secret that should simplify your process modeling: There are only three ways a process can start.

1. On external request. We just talked about that one. Model the requester as a black-box pool with a message flow to the process Message start event. This is the most frequent occurrence. The start message indicates the process instance.

    In Figure 2-11, the requester is external. Even though there are intermediate interactions with the process, they are on an exception basis.

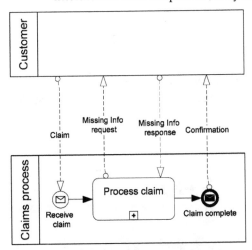

Figure 2-11. External participant as black-box pool

2. Initiation by internal task performer. In Figure 2-12, the Requisitioner has specific tasks to perform in the process, preparing the requisition and justification documents, securing management approval, and verifying the purchased items arrive in good order and are OK to pay. Normally in this case you would use a *None start event*, as shown here, signifying manual start by a task performer.

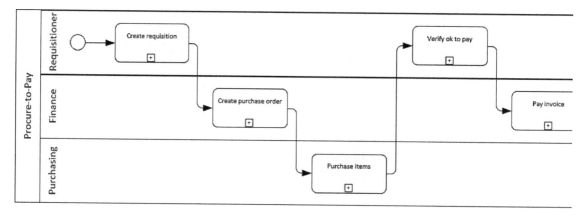

Figure 2-12. Start on internal request

3. A recurring process. Regardless of whether it is started automatically or manually, a recurring process is modeled with a Timer start event, with the clock icon, labeled with the frequency of occurrence (Figure 2-13).

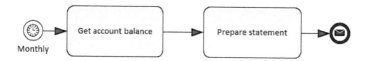

Figure 2-13. A recurring process

With Timer start, there is no requester pool, and the instance is a single occurrence. For example, in Figure 2-13 the instance is a monthly occurrence. All activities in this process must be performed once a month.

The Top-Level Diagram

Let's take another look at what we have created so far in our Order process (Figure 2-14). At this point, we have a simple but fairly complete top-level BPMN diagram. In this diagram, the details of *Fulfill Order* are hidden, but we can drill down to see the child-level expansion in a separate hyperlinked diagram.

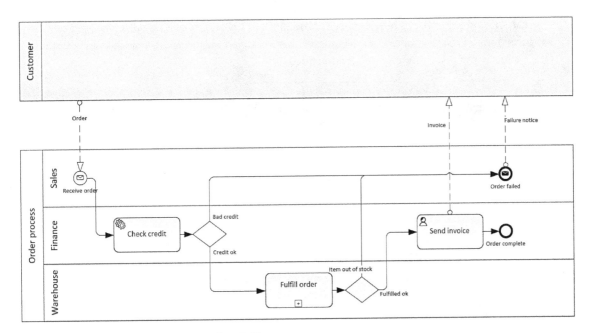

Figure 2-14. Order process, top-level diagram

But note how much this top-level diagram reveals about the process. We see that the instance represents an order, since it starts upon receipt of the *Order* message. It has *two end states*, *Order complete* and *Order failed*. The source of order failure is either the Customer's bad credit or the order item is out of stock. We see the messages returned to the Customer, either an *Invoice* if the order is successful or a *Failure notice* if it is not. In Method and Style, this basic process-level information should always be easily visible from the top-level diagram.

The Level 1 Working Set

At this point, believe it or not, you've seen all the primary elements, or *flow nodes*, in the BPMN *Level 1 working set*. It's officially called the *Descriptive Process Modeling Conformance Subclass*, but everyone knows it as Level 1. The Level 1 working set represents shapes mostly carried over from traditional flowcharting and thus familiar to business users. You can model many of your real-world processes without ever going beyond Level 1.

Let's review the Level 1 flow nodes. The diagrams up to now have been created using Vizi Modeler, the Visio add-in from itp commerce. Here I'll show you how the shapes look in both that tool and Trisotech, a cloud/browser-based tool, to give an idea of the kind of differences in notation to expect with BPMN tools.

Activity

An *activity* represents a unit of work performed in the process. It is always represented by a rounded rectangle, and should be labeled Verb-object. It is the only BPMN element that has a *performer*. Every activity is either a *task* or a *subprocess*. A *task* is *atomic*, meaning it has no internal subparts described by the process model; a *subprocess* is *compound*, meaning it has subparts defined in the model. Those subparts are modeled as a *child-level process*, an activity flow from start to one or more explicit end states.

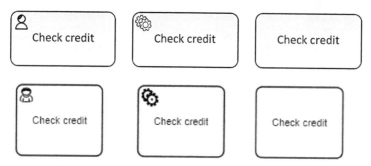

Figure 2-15. User task, service task, untyped task

BPMN defines eight task types, but Level 1 just includes these three (Figure 2-15).

- A *user task* (left), with the head-and-shoulders icon, means a task performed by a person.

- A *service task* (center), with the gears icon, means an automated activity. Automated means when the sequence flow arrives, the task starts automatically, with zero human intervention. If a person has to just click a button and the rest is automatic, that is a User task, not a Service task.

- An untyped *task* (right), with no task type icon, simply means the task type is unspecified. When all tasks in a diagram are user tasks, it is OK to omit the task type icons.

A *subprocess* is a compound activity, with subparts that can be described as a child-level process. A subprocess can be represented in multiple ways in the diagram. A *collapsed subprocess* is drawn in the parent-level diagram using an activity shape with a [+] symbol at the bottom center; the child-level expansion is normally drawn in a separate hyperlinked diagram.

Alternatively, the parent and child levels may be drawn in the same diagram using an *expanded subprocess* shape enclosing the child elements, called *inline expansion*. Keep in mind that a sequence flow may not cross the process level boundary (Figure 2-16). The incoming and outgoing sequence flows must connect to the subprocess boundary, and there should be start and end events inside the expanded subprocess.

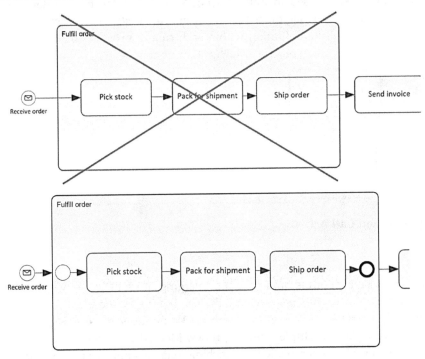

Figure 2-16. A sequence flow cannot cross subprocess boundary.

There is no semantic difference between inline and hierarchical expansion. When the sequence flow arrives at the subprocess in the parent level, the process immediately continues out of the start event at child level. And when it reaches the child-level end event, it resumes on the sequence flow out of the subprocess in the parent level.

A subprocess start event must have a None trigger. You may not use a Message start event or Timer start event in a subprocess. That is a BPMN rule, not a style rule. The reason is that the start of the subprocess is not triggered by an event; it is *always* triggered by the same thing – arrival of the incoming sequence flow[10].

---

[10] This is true for a regular subprocess, but an *event subprocess* is an exception handler triggered by an event. Event subprocesses beyond both Level 1 and Level 2, but are occasionally useful. They are discussed in Chapter 7.

Call Activity

BPMN distinguishes a *subprocess* from a *call activity*, which looks almost the same but with a thick border (Figure 2-17). This distinction has to do with whether the subprocess detail – the child-level expansion – is defined within the parent-level process model or independently. If you have some subprocess that is used in multiple processes, it is often best to define it independently – as a completely separate process model – and then *call* it from each process that uses it, rather than replicate the definition within each calling process. In the calling process, a *call activity*, links to the called process, which acts as its child level.

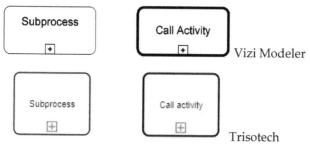

Figure 2-17. Subprocess and Call Activity

Gateway

A *gateway*, the diamond shape, controls branching and merging of sequence flows. BPMN defines several types of gateways, distinguished by the symbol inside the diamond. Each type specifies a different branching or merging behavior. While the spec allows gateways with both multiple incoming and multiple outgoing flows, Method and Style does not. A style rule says a gateway must be either explicitly branching (one incoming sequence flow) or merging (one outgoing sequence flow).

The most common is the XOR gateway, with no symbol inside. You sometimes see it with an X inside. There is no difference in meaning; the spec just says pick one convention and use it consistently, so we'll use the one with no symbol inside.

Each outgoing sequence flow, or gate, represents a data condition, which could be true or false. In any process instance, only one gate of an XOR gateway has a true condition, and this is the path selected. Method and Style adds a constraint: The condition tested is always the *end state of the prior activity*, indicated by the gate label. When the prior activity is a subprocess, the end states are also indicated by the child-level end events. This leads to the style rule that *the count of gates must equal the count of child-level end states, and their names must match as well*.

When a gateway has exactly two gates, an alternative labeling is allowed, in which the gateway itself is labeled as the success end state with a question mark – such as *Fulfilled OK?* – and the gates are labeled *yes* and *no*. In my previous book, I tended to favor this labeling style, but now I think the "normal" way, matching each gate label to an end state, is preferable. Either way, this label matching helps the consumer of your model trace the logic from parent to child process level.

An important difference between a BPMN gateway and the diamond-shaped "decision box" in flowcharting is that *a gateway does not "make" a decision; it just tests a data condition.* A gateway cannot approve or reject, for example. You need a task to do that. Then a gateway following the task can test the decision task end state and route the subsequent flow based on the result. The left diagram in Figure 2-18 is incorrect in BPMN; the one on the right is correct.

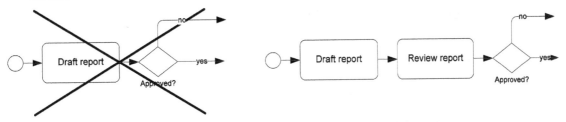

Figure 2-18. A gateway cannot *make* a decision; it only *tests* a data condition.

A *parallel gateway*, also called an *AND gateway*, has a + marker inside the diamond. A *parallel split*, with one sequence flow in and multiple sequence flows out, means that *all* of the outgoing sequence flows are to be followed in parallel, unconditionally. A *parallel join*, with multiple sequence flows in and one out, waits for all incoming sequence flows to arrive, then continues. With parallel gateways, neither the gateway nor the gates should be labeled.

Parallel paths merge downstream in a join, but they may lead to separate end events. In the latter case, each parallel path must reach an end event in order for the process level to be complete.

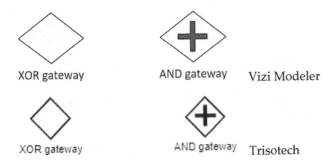

Figure 2-19. XOR gateway and AND gateway

Start Event

A *start event*, a circle with a single thin border, indicates how a process or subprocess starts. Normally a process or subprocess has a single start event. In a top-level process, the icon inside the circle, called the *trigger*, identifies the type of signal that instantiates the process.

Just as important, the trigger identifies the *meaning* of the process instance as the handling of that single triggering event.

Vizi Modeler

Trisotech

Figure 2-20. Level 1 Start events

Level 1 includes three types of start events (Figure 2-20).

A *None start event*, with no icon inside, has no trigger. In a top-level process, it normally signifies manual start by a task performer... but it could also mean the modeler has not specified the trigger. Usually None start events are unlabeled. A subprocess MUST have a *None* start event because a subprocess is not triggered by an event but by an incoming sequence flow.[11]

A *Message start event*, with the envelope icon, means that the process is triggered upon receipt of a message, an external request. The process instance represents the handling of that single request. A Message start event should be labeled *Receive [name of message]*, and the diagram should include a message flow drawn to the event. This is a style rule.

A *Timer start event*, with the clock icon, signifies a recurring process, and should be labeled to indicate frequency of occurrence, such as *Monthly*. With a Timer start event, the process instance is one of those occurrences.

End Event

An *end event*, a circle with a single thick border, indicates the end of a path in a process or subprocess. If the instance reaches an end event and no parallel paths have not yet reached an end event, the process level is complete. A black icon inside an end event, called the *result*, indicates a trigger thrown – i.e., sent – by the process when the end event is reached. Unlike start events, there is often more than one end event in a process level. In fact, Method and Style requires a separate end event for each distinct end state. If a process level has more than one end event, each must be labeled to indicate the end state, Noun-adjective or an adjective phrase.

Level 1 includes three types of end events (Figure 2-21).

---

[11] Event subprocesses, discussed in Chapter 7, are an exception; they have triggered start events.

None   Message   Terminate   Vizi Modeler

None   Message   Terminate   Trisotech

Figure 2-21. Level 1 end events

A *None* end event (no icon inside) signifies that no trigger signal is thrown when the end event is reached.

A *Message* end event (black envelope icon) signifies that a message is sent upon reaching the end event. A message flow should be drawn from the event. Even though it sends a message, a Message end event should always be labeled to indicate the end state, e.g., *Order rejected*, not *Send rejection notice*.

A *Terminate* end event (bulls-eye icon) is a special case used to resolve deadlocks at a join, such as the upper diagram in Figure 2-22.

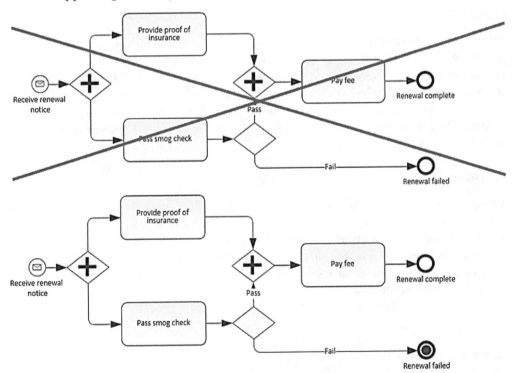

Figure 2-22. Terminate end event

If *Pass Smog Check* fails, one path goes to the end state *Renewal failed*, but the process is not complete because a parallel path is waiting at the join. This model is deadlocked, because the join can never complete. Terminate resolves this problem. Reaching Terminate in a process level immediately ends the process level even if other parallel paths have not yet completed. Reaching Terminate in a subprocess only ends that subprocess, not the parent-level process.

You sometimes see Terminate used simply to indicate an exception end state, but this is incorrect. Terminate should be reserved for terminating exceptions originating in a parallel block.

Sequence Flow

Sequence flow, drawn in the diagram as a solid line connector, represents the sequential execution of process steps: When the node at the tail of a sequence flow completes, the node at the arrowhead is enabled to start. In an executable process, it represents an actual flow of control: When the tail node completes, the arrowhead node is automatically started by the process engine. The only elements that can connect to the tail or head of a sequence flow are activities, gateways, and events, called *flow nodes*.

Figure 2-23. Sequence flow

All activities, gateways, and events must lie on a continuous chain of sequence flows, within a process level, from start event to end event. So-called "implicit" start and end nodes that violate this rule, technically allowed by the spec, and not allowed by Method and Style. The chain of sequence flows is confined within a process level, so *a sequence flow may not cross a process or process level boundary*. This is a rule of the BPMN metamodel. Also, both ends of a sequence flow must be connected to a flow node. If one end is left unconnected, the model will not be valid.

Message Flow

Message flow, drawn in the diagram as a dashed line connector, represents one-way communication between the process and an external entity. A message flow can connect to an activity, Message event, or black-box pool. Both ends of the message flow must be connected. You may *not* connect a message flow to the boundary of a process pool; you must directly connect to an activity or event inside the pool. Also, a message flow may not connect two elements in the same process.

Figure 2-24. Message flow

Pool

A *pool* represents a process in the context of its interactions with external entities. A pool containing flow elements, called a *process pool* or *white-box pool*, should be labeled with the name of the *process,* not an organization or role. If a child process level is enclosed in a pool, the pool label should still be the name of the process, not the subprocess. A *black-box pool,* completely empty, may be used to represent the external entity. In that case, it should be labeled with the name of a *business entity or role,* such as Customer or Seller.

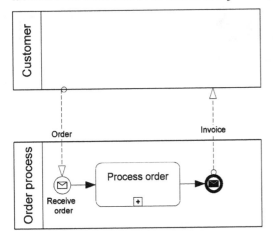

Figure 2-25. Black-box pool (top) and process pool (bottom)

Lane

A *lane* is an optional subdivision of a process or subprocess used to indicate the performer of its enclosed activities. Although BPMN allows you to draw lanes without enclosing them in a pool, some tools do not. Lane labels indicate roles or organizational units. Activities may not straddle lanes; if lanes are used in a process level, all flow nodes must be in one lane or another. Lanes are defined independently in each process level. Some levels may omit lanes, while others include them.

Data Object and Data Store

In non-executable processes, data and data flow play a secondary role in BPMN models. *Data object,* a dog-eared page icon, represents a variable in an executable process. It is of little use in non-executable process models.

Figure 2-26. Data object and data store

More useful is *data store,* a cylinder shape representing information stored in an application, database, or file, that both the process and external entities may read and write. *Shared data,* represented by a data store, provides an important alternative to message flow for passing information to a process.

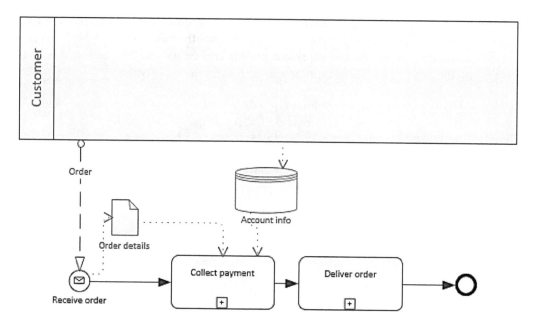

Figure 2-27. Passing information with message flow vs shared data

Figure 2-27 illustrates the difference between a message and shared data. In some e-commerce sites, the Customer's credit card information is not passed in the order message. It is stored in the Customer's account information, which is accessible to both the Customer and the order process. Here *Order* is a message. With an incoming message, the information is pushed by the external entity and the process reacts immediately upon its receipt.

In executable BPMN, the contents of the *Order* message are stored in the data object *Order details*, which is an input to the activity *Collect payment*. This detail is omitted in most process models. *Collect payment* retrieves the Customer's credit card information from the data store *Account info*. The dotted V-arrow linking to Account info is called a *data association*[12]. The arrow going into the data store signifies a create or update operation; an arrow out of the data store signifies a query/retrieve operation. So we see here the Customer updates his credit card information in the data store, and the process retrieves it with each order.

With an incoming message the process is passive and reacts to its arrival. With shared data, the process is active and retrieves the information when needed. For all practical purposes, message and shared data are the only ways information can be passed to a process, and both are used extensively in real business processes.

---

[12] Technically the spec does not allow a data association to connect to a black-box pool, but this is a bug. To avoid validation errors in a tool, you can use the regular association connector with attribute Direction = One instead. It looks identical and does not create a violation.

Text Annotation

The BPMN model as a whole and most of its individual elements each contain a *documentation* element in the XML, into which you can stuff as much information as you please, either directly or via links to external documents. These documentation elements are part of the Descriptive subclass (i.e., Level 1), meaning any tool that claims conformance is expected to be able to import and display them. However, *documentation* has no associated graphical element. In other words, it doesn't show up in the diagram.

If you want to put an annotation in the diagram itself, use *text annotation*, indicated in the diagram by a square bracket shape framing a bit of user-entered text (Figure 2-28). Text annotations are not supposed to be free-floating but attached to some graphical element via a non-directional *association*.

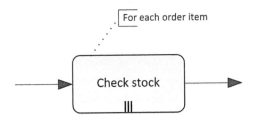

Figure 2-28. Text annotation and association

CHAPTER 3

The Method

We've now covered the full Level 1 working set, which is sufficient to handle the majority of your process modeling requirements. So we are now ready to discuss the Method.

The Method is not part of the BPMN specification. OMG proudly declares that BPMN has no official methodology, since it is intended for use by practitioners with divergent interests and skills. But Good BPMN demands some methodology, and Method and Style provides one. The Method is a systematic approach to creating Good BPMN from the detailed notes gathered in stakeholder interviews and workshops. Applying the Method cannot be done in real time as part of the workshops themselves. It is performed afterward by carefully reorganizing that information.

In my BPMN classes, students find the Method the most difficult part. Reorganizing these process details is just an inherently difficult thing to do. But beyond that, the Method asks the modeler to think about the process top-down and somewhat abstractly, which is in stark contrast to the way stakeholder information was originally gathered, concretely and bottom-up: *What happens first? What happens after that?* Etc.

Let's recall the goals of Good BPMN:

1. Correctness. Now we understand this means not only *semantic correctness* – the shapes and symbols are used correctly – but *structural correctness* as well, so that the instance of each activity corresponds 1:1 with the process instance.

2. Clarity. The process logic should be clear from the diagrams alone, without prior knowledge of how the process works or even of the terminology employed.

3. Completeness. It should be possible to tell from a single glance how the process starts, its possible end states, what the instance represents, and all interactions with external entities. The Method actually begins with this.

4. Consistency. Given the same set of process information, ideally all modelers should create (more or less) the same process model. If all members of your project team follow the Method, understanding each other's diagrams becomes a breeze. Over ten

years of teaching Method and Style, the Method has evolved to become more mechanical, more standardized in the order of its steps, and this has helped with consistency.

These goals are not achievable in the information gathered in real time in stakeholder workshops. There the challenge is simply to engage the business users and get them to talk about the process, and the business analyst or facilitator just hopes to capture it all. Thus the Method is applied afterward.

Outline of the Method

The Method has five steps. They must be followed in this order. I'll outline them here and then drill down to their details.

1. Process Model Scope

Step 1 is defining the process model scope, how the business process starts and its possible end states. In BPMN terms, Step 1 determines the process start and end events, as well as the process instance.

2. High-Level Map

Step 2, the High-Level Map, is the hardest part of the Method. The High-Level Map is just a list, not yet BPMN. Creating it requires taking all the actions mentioned in the stakeholder workshop notes and sorting them into buckets. Each bucket is going to be an activity in the top-level BPMN. We want the top-level diagram to fit on one page, so we cannot have more than 10 of these buckets. And, of course, the instance of each bucket must have 1:1 correspondence with the process instance. Any actions without that instance correspondence get put in special buckets off to the side. We need to give an activity name to each bucket, Verb-object.

And there's more to Step 2. Once we have our 10 or fewer named buckets, we ask where does the process go next once this bucket ends. The choices are limited to the other buckets or the process end states from Step 1. And if for some activities there is more than one possibility, we need to assign an end state to each possible next step.

So Step 2 generates a list of activity names and for each one a list of end state names.

3. Top-Level BPMN

Step 3 turns the High-Level Map from a list into a top-level BPMN diagram. It may seem hard on Day One of BPMN training, but fundamentally it's trivial... because all of the flow nodes have already been defined and named in Steps 1 and 2! In fact, Vizi Modeler provides a wizard that steps you through the Method as a questionnaire, and then generates the BPMN diagram automatically with one button click.

4. Child-Level Diagrams

The diagram created in Step 3 is structurally correct, but it hides most of the process details. Those are added now in Step 4. For each top-level activity with additional detail, make it a subprocess and model the details in a child-level diagram. If necessary, the child level may include subprocesses, which are expanded at a grandchild level.

5. Context Information

So far we have left out pools, lanes, message flows, and data flow. They all get added last, in Step 5. As mentioned previously, adding these earlier just slows you down and allows structural errors to creep in.

Step 1: Process Model Scope

In Step 1 we are defining the scope, or boundaries, of our process model. The key questions are these:

1. How does the process start? Remember, there are only three ways: external request, initiation by a task performer, or a recurring process. This determines the start event.

2. What does each instance of the process represent? This is normally given by the start event, as we have discussed. For a Message start event, the start message represents the instance. For a Timer start event, the instance is one of the occurrences.

3. What determines when the process instance is complete, both successfully in the normal success end state, and possibly in various exception end states? The end states determine the end events of the process.

Step 2: The High-Level Map

Step 2 is the most difficult part of the Method. Like Step 1, we are just creating a list, not yet diagramming anything. In Step 2 we want to take all the actions described as possibly occurring in the process and sort them into ten or fewer "buckets," each bucket representing a coarse-grained activity in the process. The limitation of 10 activities comes from the desire for the top-level BPMN diagram to fit on one page.

Obviously, the actions contained in one bucket occur together in time, and the instance of the activity must have 1:1 correspondence with the process instance determined in Step 1. If there are actions that do not fit that 1:1 correspondence, they need to go into one or more special buckets off to the side, representing activities in one or more separate BPMN processes. This instance alignment requirement is not Method and Style but demanded for structural correctness as defined by the BPMN metamodel.

After this sorting into buckets, you should have a list of 10 or fewer activities, each with a descriptive name, Verb-object. Now, for each activity, think about where the process instance goes next when the activity completes. The choice, by definition, is limited to the activities just defined or the process end states defined in Step 1. If there is more than one possibility, you need to enumerate the end states of the activity, Noun-adjective. If there is only one possible next step, it is not necessary to name it.

Remember, each activity end state corresponds to a distinct next step in the process. If, say, there are three possible ways an activity could end but two of those three go to the same next step, they share a common activity end state. Two next steps always means just two end states.

So the High Level Map created in Step 2 consists of a list of activity names, 10 or fewer, plus, for each activity with more than one possible next step, a list of end state names.

Scenario: Order Process

Here is a scenario we use in the training to illustrate the Method. These four paragraphs are an ultra-simplified representation of what could be 20 pages or more of notes and diagrams from the stakeholder interviews and workshops:

> "When we receive an order, first an order entry clerk enters it into the order system, which checks the stock on hand. If the item is available, it reserves the order item in inventory. If the item is not found in the order system, the process immediately ends with an item not found notice. If the item is back-ordered, meaning it's in the catalog but temporarily out of stock, we need to handle the back order.
>
> If the item is in stock, next we collect payment. First we validate the discount code. We update valid codes for the week every Sunday. Then we calculate the total price including discounts, tax and shipping, and charge the credit card number provided. If the charge is successful, we go on to fulfill the order. If charge is unsuccessful, a customer service rep contacts the customer to resolve it. Once the payment issue is resolved, we go on to fulfill the order. If it cannot be resolved, we send a rejection notice and the process ends.
>
> Handling a back order goes to a customer service rep who contacts the customer to see if they want to wait for the back order, substitute an available item, or cancel the order. The CSR updates the order system. If the customer continues the order (either waits or substitutes), we go on to collect payment, as before. If the customer cancels, the process ends with a cancellation notice.
>
> Fulfilling the order is simply packing the item (after waiting for back order, if necessary), shipping it, and sending the confirmation notice. This is the normal success end state."

Process Scope

Step 1 is defining the process scope, meaning the start and end events. How does this process start? Remember there are only three ways. This starts on receipt of an order message, so that says external request, Message start event, receiving *Order* message from black-box pool *Customer*. We name this event *Receive Order*. This also means that the process instance is an order, so every activity in this process must be performed once per order.

The second part of Step 1 is defining the process end states. How does this process end? If we read the scenario carefully we see there are four different ways, each returning a different final status message:

- *Order complete*, the success end state

- *Order item not found*, if we cannot find the order item in our system

- *Order rejected*, if the credit card payment fails

- *Order cancelled*, if the item is back-ordered and the Customer doesn't want to wait or substitute an in-stock item.

There are a lot of other things happening in the scenario, but these are the only four times where it says the process ends. So now we have specified our start event and four end events.

High-Level Map

Step 2 is defining the High-Level Map, a list of process activities and their end states. Normally we want to sort all the actions contained in this scenario into 10 or fewer buckets, but because of the simplicity of our scenario, here we limit it to 4 buckets only. The mindset of Method Step 2 is aggregating actions from the scenario into a smaller number of coarse-grained activities, each named in the form Verb-object.

There is no single "correct" answer. Here are my four activities:

- *Enter order*, described in the first paragraph, in which the order information is entered into the order system, which either reserves it from stock or indicates out of stock. There is also the possibility that the ordered item cannot be found in the order system.

- *Collect payment*, described in the second paragraph, in which the credit card is charged. If that fails, a representative contacts the customer and tries to resolve the problem.

- *Handle back-order*, described in the third paragraph, in which a representative contacts the customer to determine whether to wait for the item to come in, substitute an available item, or possibly cancel the order.

- *Fulfill order*, described in the last paragraph, in which the order is packed and shipped, along with a confirmation.

One of the actions mentioned in the scenario, updating the valid discount codes, is performed weekly not with every order, so it is not part of *Collect payment* or any other activity in this process. It goes into a special bucket off to the side, part of a process performed weekly.

We're not done yet with Step 2. Now we need to consider the scenario details for each activity and ask, *Where does the process go next after this activity completes?* It can only be one of the four activities (including redoing the current activity) or one of the three process end events. If there is more than one possibility, we need to enumerate the activity end states.

For *Enter Order*, we see that if it's in stock we go next to *Collect payment*. If it's out of stock, we go next to *Handle back-order*. And if we cannot find the order item in the order system, we go next to the process end state *Order item not found*. So we need to name three activity end states, one per next step. Mine are listed in the table below.

Table 1. End states of *Enter order*

End state of *Enter order*	Next step
Item in stock	Collect payment
Item back-ordered	Handle back-order
Item not found	Order item not found

For *Collect payment*, we see that if the charge ultimately succeeds, we go next to *Fulfill order*, and if it ultimately does not succeed, we go next to the process end state *Order rejected*. So that means two end states.

Table 2. End states of *Collect payment*

End state of Collect payment	Next step
Charge OK	Fulfill order
Charge failed	Order rejected

For *Handle back-order*, the customer can give one of three responses – wait, substitute, or cancel – but two of those three go to the same next step, *Collect payment*. So there are just two end states, one per distinct next step.

Table 3. End states of *Handle back-order*

End states of *Handle back-order*	Next step
Order continued	Collect payment
Order cancelled	Order cancelled

Fulfill order always goes to the same next step, *Order complete*, so there is no need to name its end state.

This completes Step 2 of the Method. We just have a list of activities, end states, and next steps.

Top-Level Process Diagram

Step 3 of the Method is turning the High-Level Map into the top-level BPMN diagram. Students find it hard at first but it's really easy, because everything you need has already been defined and named in Step 1 and Step 2: start event, end events, activities, and gateways. An activity with three end states must be followed in the diagram by a gateway with three gates, each matching one of the end states.

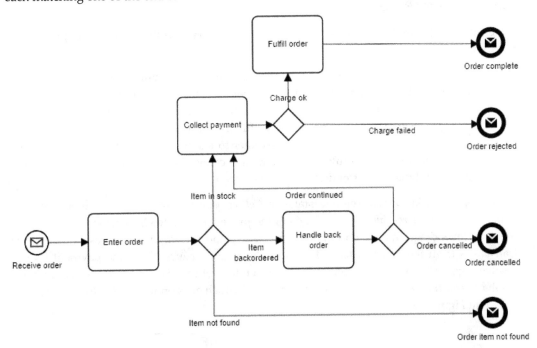

Figure 3-1. Top-level BPMN diagram, following the High-Level Map

The result is Figure 3-1. Study that for a minute, and compare it to the High-Level Map. We do not yet have pools, lanes, message flows or data flow, and most of the detail from the scenario is not yet included, but the diagram generated in this way is structurally correct and properly labeled according to Method and Style.

Child-Level Diagrams

In Step 4 of the Method, details of each top-level activity are captured in child-level diagrams. Again, there should be no more than 10 activities in each diagram. The child-level diagram could contain collapsed subprocesses, which would be expanded in grandchild-level diagrams, and there is no theoretical limit to the number of process levels. In practice, most process models are no more than three levels deep.

If the top-level activities were drawn as tasks, first convert them to collapsed subprocesses. Most BPMN tools allow you to do this conversion. Then create a child-level diagram, hyperlinked to the subprocess, to describe its details. (The mechanics of creating the linked child-level diagram differ from tool to tool, but it is a standard feature of BPMN tools.)

The child-level expansion must have a None start event. The end events of the child level were already determined in Step 2. They are the end states of the top-level activity. Every path in the child level must terminate in one of those end events.

Scenario: Order Process

For example, let's do this for the activity *Collect payment*. Here is the relevant paragraph from the scenario:

> "... next we collect payment. First we validate the discount code. We update valid codes for the week every Sunday. Then we calculate the total price including discounts, tax and shipping, and charge the credit card number provided. If the charge is successful, we go on to fulfill the order. If charge is unsuccessful, a customer service rep contacts the customer to resolve it. Once the payment issue is resolved, we go on to fulfill the order. If it cannot be resolved, we send a rejection notice and the process ends."

From Step 2, we know that the end states of *Collect payment* are *Charge OK*, which leads to *Fulfill order*, and *Charge failed*, which leads to the process end state *Order rejected*. All paths in the child-level diagram must end in one of those two end states. This requires a bit of mental translation from the scenario text. For example, when it says, "Once the payment issue is resolved, go on to fulfill the order," you need to interpret that as "Once the payment issue is resolved, end the child level in the state *Charge ok*," which goes on to *Fulfill order*. The result is shown in Figure 3-2.

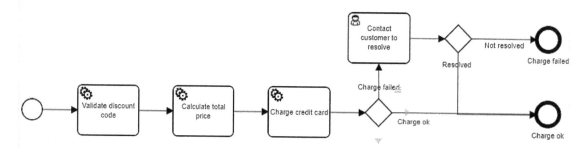

Figure 3-2. Child-level diagram of *Collect payment*

Context Information

At the end of Step 4 you should have all process details captured in a hierarchical set of BPMN diagrams, but without pools, lanes, message flow, or data flow. All of that "context information" is added at the end, in Step 5 of the Method. Adding it earlier just slows you down and makes it easier to introduce structural errors.

The only bit of context information required by Method and Style is message flow. Style rules require that any Message event or any activity that sends or receives a message must have a message flow attached. The other context information is optional. Add it if you wish.

Unlike most of the Method, which progresses top-down, adding message flows proceeds bottom-up, starting from the lowest process level that sends or receives a message. In a child-level diagram, the "other" end of the message flow must be a black-box pool, so start by inserting that in the diagram, and then draw the message flow. A message flow always must be connected at both head and tail ends. Once you've added all the message flows and black-box pools in the child-level diagram, you need to replicate them in the parent-level diagram. The message flow and black-box pool names must match in the parent and child diagrams.

Scenario: Order Process

In Figure 3-3, the Customer pool and message flows have been added to the child level of *Collect payment*. Because a message is a one-way communication, a conversation like *Contact customer* would be modeled as a pair of messages, a request and a response.

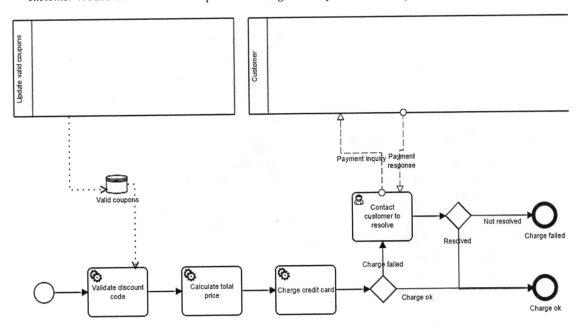

Figure 3-3. Message flow and shared data in *Collect payment* child level

Figure 3-3 also illustrates handling of the extra bucket from Step 2, the weekly update of discount codes. Updating the codes occurs weekly, so that action occurs in a process that runs once a week. We don't really know what else is in that process, so we model it abstractly as a black-box pool, *Update valid coupon*. That process interacts with our order process via shared data, modeled as the data store *Valid coupons*. The data association into the data store represents the weekly update. The data association out of the data store represents the query of valid codes from the process activity *Validate discount code.* Ideally, if you have the space in the diagram, these shared data interactions should be replicated from child to parent level as well.

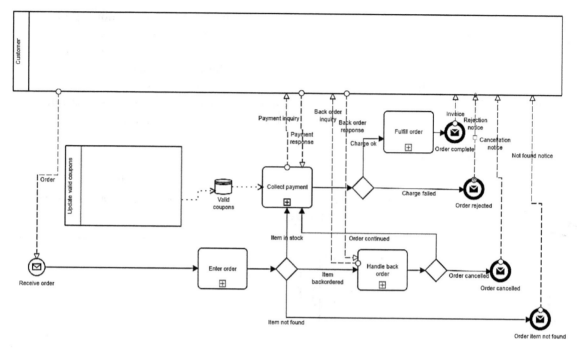

Figure 3-4. Top level with message flows

The top-level diagram with replicated message flows and shared data is shown in Figure 3-4. Style rule validation checks that message flow and black-box pool names match in parent and child-level diagrams.

Step 5 also is where lanes are added, if you so choose. If lanes are not used, it is best not to enclose the child-level flow nodes in a pool. If you use lanes, some tools force you to enclose them in a pool. Remember, in a child level the pool label must be the process name, not the subprocess name. This comes from the BPMN metamodel, not Method and Style. Lanes are defined independently in each process level.

Method Wizard

The Method is an attempt to systematically address the chaotic nature of process information gathered in stakeholder workshops and interviews. The Method asks specific questions in a particular order. How does the process start and end? What are its top-level activities? Et cetera. In principle, one should be able to generate the complete BPMN model from the answers to these questions.

The Method Wizard in Vizi Modeler does just that. Via a questionnaire, Step 1 in the wizard determines the start and end events (Figure 3-5).

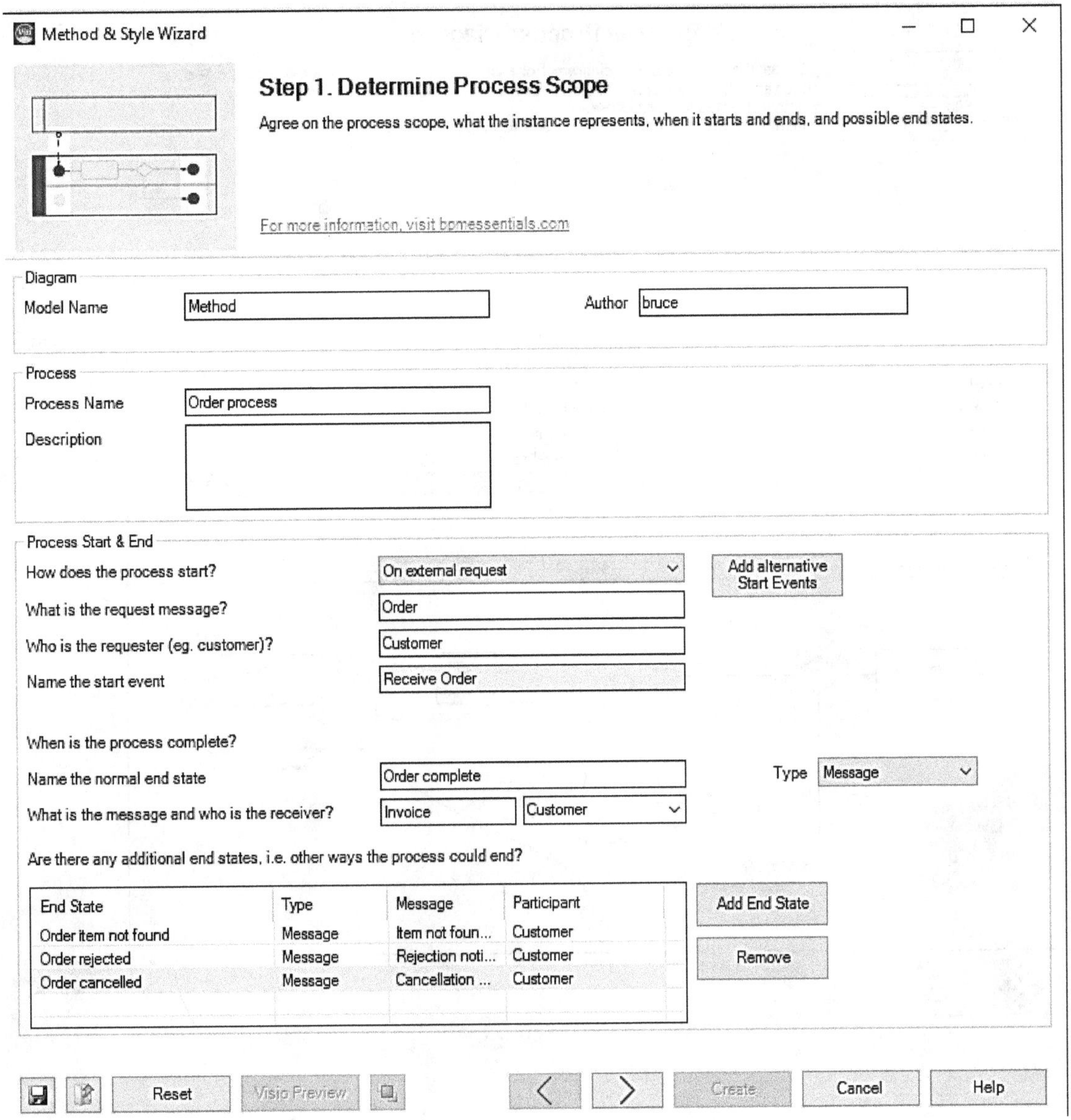

Method & Style Wizard　　　　　　　　　　　　　　— □ ✕

Step 1. Determine Process Scope

Agree on the process scope, what the instance represents, when it starts and ends, and possible end states.

For more information, visit bpmessentials.com

Diagram

Model Name | Method　　　　　　　　　　Author | bruce

Process

Process Name | Order process

Description |

Process Start & End

How does the process start? | On external request ∨ | Add alternative Start Events

What is the request message? | Order

Who is the requester (eg. customer)? | Customer

Name the start event | Receive Order

When is the process complete?

Name the normal end state | Order complete　　Type | Message ∨

What is the message and who is the receiver? | Invoice | Customer ∨

Are there any additional end states, i.e. other ways the process could end?

End State	Type	Message	Participant
Order item not found	Message	Item not foun...	Customer
Order rejected	Message	Rejection noti...	Customer
Order cancelled	Message	Cancellation ...	Customer

Add End State

Remove

Reset | Visio Preview | < > | Create | Cancel | Help

Figure 3-5. Vizi Modeler Method Wizard, Step 1

In Steps 2 and 3, you enter the names of the activities, their end states, and the next step for each activity end state (Figure 3-6). The wizard gives you an instant preview of the resulting BPMN. Steps 4 and 5 define child-level diagrams and message flows. Clicking Create then automatically generates a complete, properly constructed BPMN diagram.

Step 3. Top-Level Process Diagram

Create the top-level BPMN diagram. For each activity, determine which one comes next.
If an activity has multiple end states, define a target for each end state. A gateway will be drawn following the activity that tests the end states.
Mark the targets on which parallel flows need to be merged.

For more information, visit bpmessentials.com

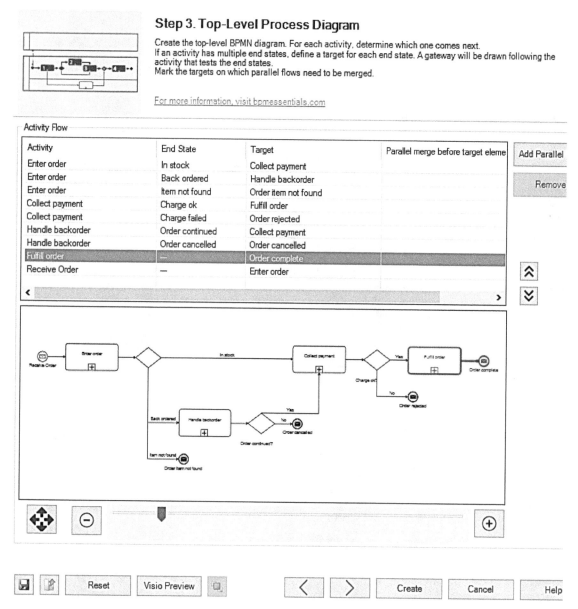

Activity Flow

Activity	End State	Target	Parallel merge before target eleme
Enter order	In stock	Collect payment	
Enter order	Back ordered	Handle backorder	
Enter order	Item not found	Order item not found	
Collect payment	Charge ok	Fulfill order	
Collect payment	Charge failed	Order rejected	
Handle backorder	Order continued	Collect payment	
Handle backorder	Order cancelled	Order cancelled	
Fulfill order	—	Order complete	
Receive Order	—	Enter order	

Add Parallel

Remove

Reset | Visio Preview | Create | Cancel | Help

Figure 3-6. Vizi Modeler Method Wizard, Step 3

Structural Correctness

A key motivation for the Method is to ensure that your BPMN is structurally correct. We've discussed one aspect of that, which is instance alignment between the process and its component activities. But there is a second aspect, as well, which involves the notion of top-level and child-level diagrams or pages.

Technically, BPMN models are data structures that must conform to the BPMN metamodel, but they are created simply by assembling shapes into diagrams. In that data structure, each diagram or "page" of the model must be either a *top-level page* or a *child-level page*. There is no "in-between". *A page containing one or more top-level processes is, by definition, a top-level page.* In the data structure, that page is associated with a *process*, or if the page has pool shapes, a *collaboration*, i.e., interactions between the process and external entities. *A page displaying the contents of a subprocess is, by definition, a child-level page.* In the data structure, that page is linked to the subprocess element on the parent page.

Possibly you can see the potential conflict here. A child-level page may not contain flow nodes of any process other than the one containing the subprocess in the parent level. That means, in turn, that *a message flow on a child page must connect to a black-box pool.* Connecting it to a flow node of another process is a structural error.

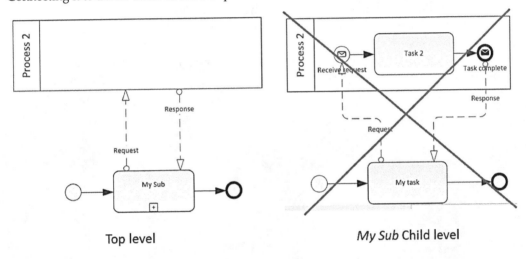

Top level   *My Sub* Child level

Figure 3-7. A child-level diagram may not contain flow nodes of another process

This conflict is illustrated in Figure 3-7. The top-level diagram on the left includes a subprocess *My Sub* with message flows to *Process 2*. The child-level diagram of *My Sub* on the right may not contain flow nodes of any process other than the one containing *My Sub*, so the diagram on the right is structurally invalid. Message flows from *My task* in the child-level diagram must connect to the black-box pool *Process 2*, not to flow nodes within the white-box pool *Process 2*.

Method Recap

We've now covered the Method. Let's review the steps:

1. Define the process scope, how the process starts and ends, what the instance represents, and possible end states. This specifies the process start and end events.

2. Sort all process actions into buckets in order to create a high-level map, enumerating the major activities, ten or fewer, each aligned with the process instance. Think about the possible next steps when each activity completes. If more than one, enumerate its end states, Noun-adjective, one per next step. In the end you have a list of activity names, Verb-object, each with a list of end state names and their associated next step.

3. Create the top-level BPMN diagram. All the flow nodes have been defined and named already from Steps 1 and 2: the activities, gateways and gates (one per end state), start and end events. All you need to do is draw it.

4. Make any top-level activity with additional details a subprocess, and expand it in a child-level diagram. The child-level end events must be the end states from Step 2.

5. Add context information: pools and message flows, lanes, and shared data connections. Draw message flows starting from the lowest level they occur, and then replicate each one in the parent-level diagram. Ultimately, the top-level diagram includes all the message flows and black-box pools involved with the process. Also replicate any shared data connections from child to parent level. Lanes, if used, should be added in Step 5 as well.

CHAPTER 4

BPMN Style

The Method helps you establish consistency in the structure of your BPMN models, but by itself it does not ensure that your diagrams are Good BPMN. The rules of the BPMN specification won't do that, either. Good BPMN also requires applying additional conventions that I call *BPMN style*.

At one time I referred to BPMN style as recommended "best practices," since these conventions, after all, are not required by the BPMN 2.0 specification. But in my BPMN training today they are called *rules*, of equal importance to the rules of the spec. That is why we limit the tools used our training to those that have style rule validation built in, like Vizi Modeler, Trisotech, and Signavio. This has made a huge difference in both student model quality and learning of the style rules.

The Basic Principle of BPMN Style

The basic principle of BPMN Style is simply this: *The process logic should be clear from the diagram alone, even to those who do not already know it.* That's the essence of Good BPMN.

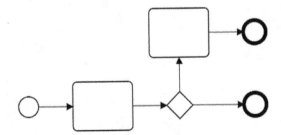

Figure 4-1. A "valid" but meaningless process

Consider the process model shown in Figure 4-1. What process logic does it communicate? I would say basically none at all, so it is definitely not Good BPMN. But it is completely *valid* according to the BPMN 2.0 specification. If you check it in a tool that just validates against the rules of the spec, such as the Visio Pro native BPMN editor, it shows zero errors, perfect.

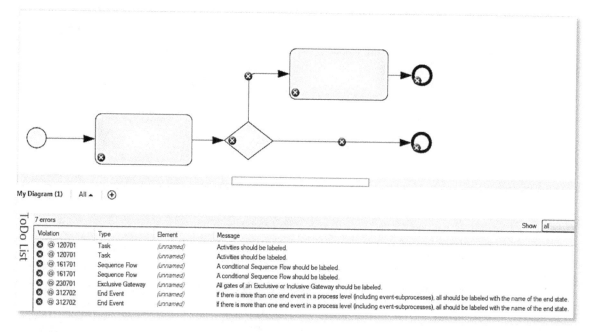

Figure 4-2. Style rule violations in Figure 4-1, Vizi Modeler

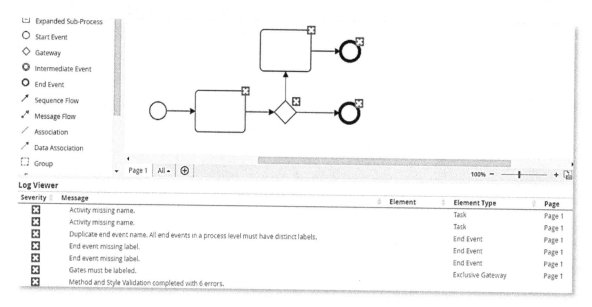

Figure 4-3. Style rule violations in Figure 4-1, Trisotech

That is why style rule validation is so important. Here is the same model validated in Vizi Modeler (Figure 4-2) and Trisotech (Figure 4-3): several style errors! These all have to do with missing labels, but style rules check other things as well. Of course, the diagram must also obey the official rules of the BPMN spec.

While the basic flow node shape – activity, gateway, or event – roughly defines its meaning, its precise behavior is specified by icons, markers, and labels... all of which are called "optional" by the spec. So many style rules simply come down to this: If BPMN can provide more precise meaning through an icon, marker, or label, *use it!*

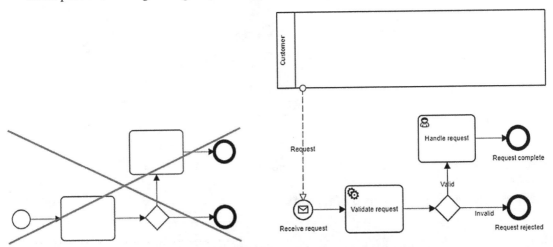

Figure 4-4. Icons, labels, and other "optional" notation communicate important meaning

Figure 4-4 illustrates it well. The flow nodes are identical in both diagrams, but the one on the right, with icons, labels, and other optional elements such as message flow, communicates meaning, while the one on the left does not.

The Most Important Style Rules

A number of style rules are basic principles of composition, while others are specific rules of usage supporting validation in a tool. The important style rules applicable to Level 1 modeling are listed below.

Make models hierarchical, with no more than 10 activities per page.

The goal is to ensure that each diagram fits on a single page. The number ten is somewhat arbitrary, but it's what the style rule checks. We want the top-level diagram to reveal in one glance all the essential process-level information: how the process starts, its possible end states, what the instance represents, and all interactions with external entities.

The diagram shown in Figure 4-5, from a document called BPMN by Example on the OMG website, is a good example of how not to do it. If you try to squeeze it down to a single page, you cannot even read the text. How many end states does this process have? Most students say 4, but the actual answer is 2, and they are not even labeled... so they could even represent the same end state.

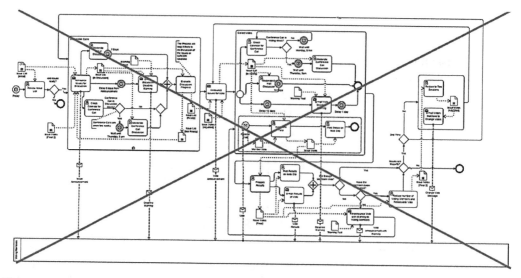

Figure 4-5. A process diagram should contain no more than 10 activities

Model external requester as a black-box pool

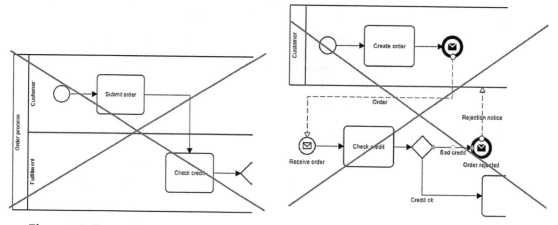

Figure 4-6. External requester should not be a lane in the process or a process pool

A common beginner mistake is to make an external process requester a lane within the process, such as the left diagram in Figure 4-6. External requesters must be outside the process, by definition, and should be modeled as a black-box pool.

Other modelers make the requester a pool but have a hard time leaving it empty. They are seemingly compelled to put something inside it, as in the right diagram. But that is also incorrect. The requester's process does not end when the request is sent. If it did, it could not receive subsequent messages, such as *Rejection notice*. This is why message flows may not connect to the boundary of a process pool. The correct way to model it is shown in Figure 4-7.

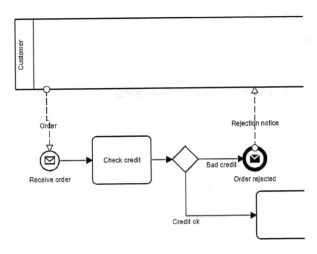

Figure 4-7. Model external requester as a black-box pool

Model process activity performers as lanes within a single process pool, not as separate pools.

A pool stands for a process (or abstract external entity), not an actor within the process. BPM as a management discipline asks you to understand the business from an end-to-end process perspective, but *separate pools mean multiple independent processes*. You should model an end-to-end process as a single BPMN process… if you can. The reason that sometimes you cannot is when the instances of each pool do not have 1:1 correspondence.

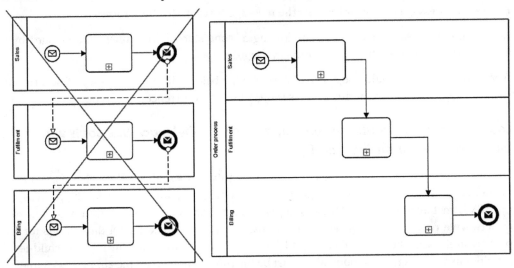

Figure 4-8. Model task performers as lanes not separate pools

The left diagram in Figure 4-8, with *Sales, Fulfillment,* and *Billing* in separate pools, is incorrect. We know that the instances align 1:1 because they are chained by message flow, where one instance of *Sales* triggers one instance of *Fulfillment*, which in turn triggers one instance of *Billing*. The diagram on the right is correct. These organizational units are lanes in a single process, not separate pools.

Use the trigger icon on a start event to indicate how the process starts and the meaning of the process instance.

Most processes are initiated by external request. In that case, the process should have a Message start event with attached message flow and labeled "Receive [name of message]". A Message start (Figure 4-9, right) means that a new instance of the process is created when the message is received. The instance of this process is the start message.

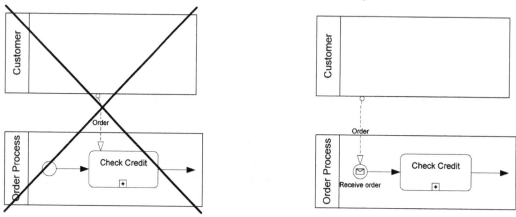

Figure 4-9. Message start event means the message instantiates the process

Receiving the message in an activity following a None start (left) implies manual start by a task performer, followed by a wait for the message.

A recurring process should use a Timer start event, labeled with the frequency of occurrence, such as *Daily*. An instance of this process is one of those occurrences.

Label process pools with the name of a process; label black-box pools with a participant role or business entity.

Labeling black-box pools using generic role or entity names like Seller, Manufacturer, or Lender is good practice, but process pools should be labeled with the name of the process. In the BPMN metamodel, a pool stands for a participant in an interaction between two processes or between a process and some abstract external entity. The process pool thus stands for the process itself, and the pool label should be the process name. If you enclose child-level activities in a pool, again the pool label must be the process name, not the subprocess name.

Label activies Verb-object, to indicate an action.

For example, *Check credit* is a good name for an activity. *Credit check*, a Noun phrase, describes a function or capability, not an action. *Credit OK*, Noun-adjective, describes a state, a good name for a gate or end event but not an activity.

Indicate distinct end states of a process or subprocess with separate end events, and label them to indicate the end state, Noun-adjective or adjective phrase.

Each end event signifies a distinct end state, and should be labeled Noun-adjective to describe that end state, where the Noun typically is the instance, such as *Order complete* or *Order rejected*. If the end event sends a message, the rule still holds, so *Send rejection notice* is not a good end event name; it still should be *Order rejected*. If a process level has only one end event, it does not need to be labeled. *End* is never a good end event name.

In a top-level process, the number of end states is up to the modeler's discretion, with the exception that success and failure should not share a single end event (Figure 4-10).

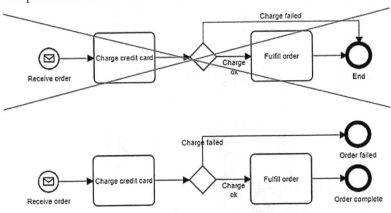

Figure 4-10. Represent distinct end states with separate end events, labeled with the end state

In a subprocess, the number of end states is the number of distinct next steps in the process. If the subprocess could end in three different ways but two of them lead to the same next step, in Method and Style they represent the same end state, and should be represented by a single end event. Again, the end event label should be Noun-adjective, indicating the end state.

The count of subprocess end states should match the count of gates in an XOR gateway following the subprocess

An XOR gateway should always follow a single activity and test the activity end state. Each gate of the gateway leads to a separate next step, and the number of activity end states is the number of next steps. When the preceding activity is a subprocess, style rules check that the count of gates equals the count of subprocess end events.

For example, the top diagram in Figure 4-11 is incorrect: two end events but no gateway. The modeler possibly thought that Terminate ends the process, but it only ends *Check credit*. The middle diagram is also incorrect: one end event but two gates. The bottom diagram is correct. It's very simple: the count of gates must equal the count of end events.

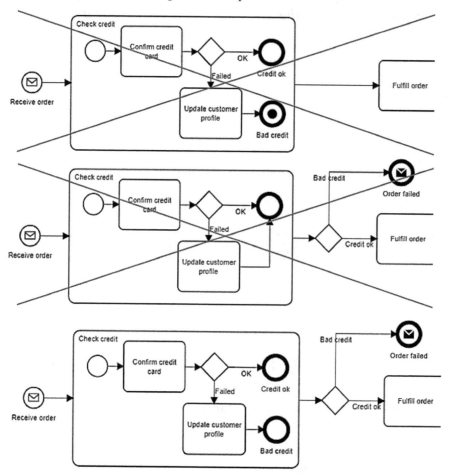

Figure 4-11. The count of gates on XOR gateway must equal the count of end states of preceding subprocess.

Match labeling of parent-level gateway and child-level end states.

Not only must the count of gates match the count of end states, but the labels must match as well. The basic rule is that each gate label must match an end state label (Figure 4-12, top). In the special case of exactly two gates and two end states, the modeler may use an alternative labeling (Figure 4-12, bottom), in which the gateway itself is labeled with the success end state followed by a question mark, and the gates are labeled *yes* and *no*.

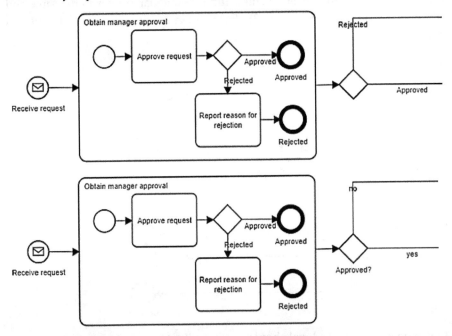

Figure 4-12. XOR gateway labeling must match end states

Two end events in a process level should not have the same name.

This follows from the previous rules. End events with the same name refer to the same end state, and thus should be combined (Figure 4-13). Each end event should represent a distinct end state, leading to a distinct next step.

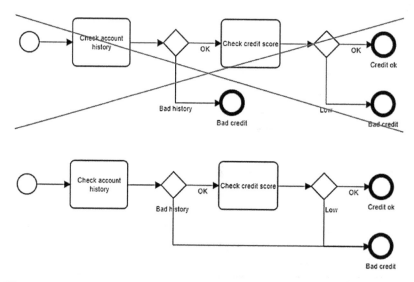

Figure 4-13. End events in a process level should not have the same name

Show message flow with all Message events, and label them correctly.

In the BPMN spec, message flows are optional, and even in some illustrations in this book, where they do not add value I may not show them. But in a real, finished BPMN model, you need to show the message flow connected to any Message event or activity that sends or receives a message. The message flow must be labeled with the name of the message, a Noun.

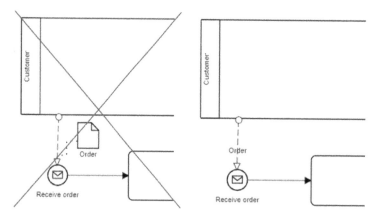

Figure 4-14. Show message flow with all Message events, labeled with name of message

Match message flows in parent- and child-level diagrams.

The count and labels of message flows should match at parent and child levels. In the Method, we start with the child level diagram and replicate the message flows (and black-box pools) in the parent-level diagram (Figure 4-15, Figure 4-16).

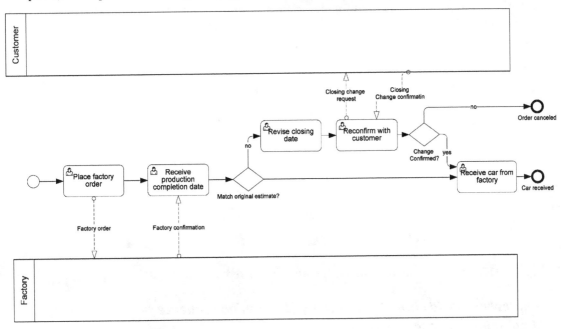

Figure 4-15. *Order car from factory,* **child level**

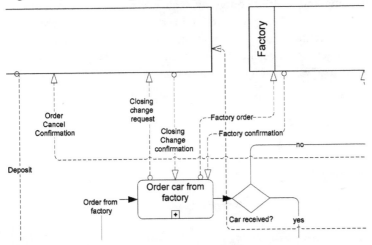

Figure 4-16. Message flows replicated in parent-level diagram

Implicit start and end nodes are not allowed.

An activity or gateway with no incoming sequence flow is called an *implicit start node*, and one with on outgoing sequence flow is called an *implicit end node*. In the spec they are allowed under specific circumstances, but most of the time they are not. Method and Style is less ambiguous: Implicit start and end nodes are never allowed. All flow nodes must lie on a continuous chain of sequence flows, within one process level, leading from a start event to an end event.

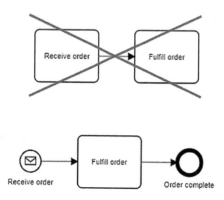

Figure 4-17. Implicit start and end nodes are not allowed

A gateway should either be branching (1 incoming sequence flow) or merging (1 outgoing sequence flow)

A gateway with multiple incoming and multiple outgoing sequence flows is allowed by the spec, but its meaning is ambiguous. Does the symbol inside the diamond define the branching or merging behavior? Method and Style is clear: Gateways must be explicitly branching or merging. That is, they must have either one incoming or one outgoing sequence flow. To merge and then branch, use two gateways (Figure 4-18).

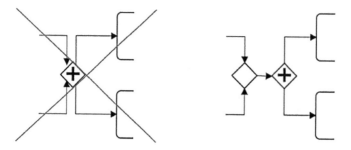

Figure 4-18. Gateways must be explicitly branching or merging

CHAPTER 5

DMN and Decision Tasks

Bad BPMN: Embedded Decision Logic

Another type of Bad BPMN, illustrated by Figure 5-1, is all too common: *decision logic*, sometimes called *business logic*, modeled as a chain of gateways in BPMN. Here the process is determining whether to approve, deny, or refer for further research an insurance claim. If you examine the diagram, you can see that the claim is approved if the policy is active, coverage for the claim is available, the claim amount is less than or equal to $1000, the risk category is Low, the customer has no previous claims, and the policy has been in force over 32 days, or it is approved by human adjudication.

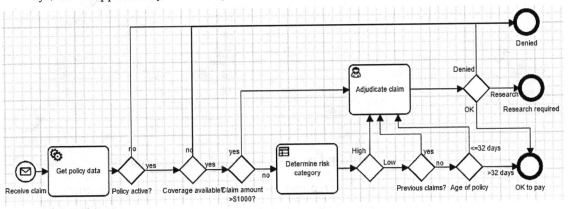

Figure 5-1. Embedding decision logic in a process model is Bad BPMN

So why is this claim adjudication process considered Bad BPMN? Obviously it is not Method and Style, since that says a gateway always follows an activity and simply tests its end state. But diagrams like this are considered bad practice by both process modeling and decision modeling experts for several reasons:

- The data elements used in the gateway logic are not defined in the process model.

- The BPMN is more complicated than necessary and hard to maintain. In practice, decision logic changes more frequently than process logic. Embedding it in the process model requires a new process version whenever the decision logic changes, e.g., the autopay claim amount threshold changes from $1000 to $1250.

- The diagram implies a particular order of evaluation of the logic, which is not really required and may not be the most efficient.

Years after BPMN 2.0 was published, a new OMG standard for business-oriented decision modeling was introduced, called *Decision Model and Notation* (DMN). DMN models are linked to BPMN through the *decision task* shape, officially called a *business rule task* in the BPMN spec. When BPMN 2.0 was published, this task type was effectively a placeholder; it had no defined semantics other than "executing a decision." In Method and Style, now we understand it to mean, execute a DMN decision.

In the BPMN metamodel, data definition is not standardized. Process data is considered something defined by developers, in tool-specific ways, in order to make the process model executable. But DMN takes a bolder stance, defining a data modeling and expression language intended for business users. This allows us to use decision tasks and DMN to turn Figure 5-1 into Good BPMN, aligned with Method and Style.

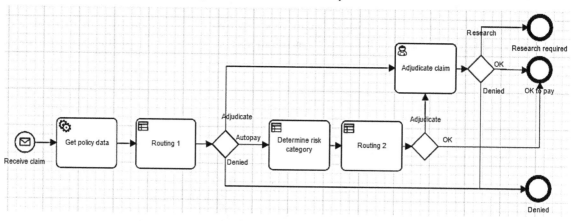

Figure 5-2. Decision tasks invoking DMN decisions enable Good BPMN

In Figure 5-2 the chains of gateways representing the decision logic have been turned into new decision tasks *Routing 1* and *Routing 2*, each followed by a single gateway that branches the flow based on the decision task's end state.

Remember that BPMN deals with *process logic*, the order of the activities. It does not address *task logic*, the internal logic of each step. But modeling the data and internal logic of a decision is precisely what DMN does.

DMN Basics

The DMN elements needed to model routing decisions like this are *decision requirements diagrams* (DRDs) and *decision tables*.

Figure 5-3 illustrates a DRD. The rectangles are called *decisions*; the ovals are called *input data*. Input data denotes values stored in some business system or process and supplied as inputs to the decision. A decision transforms the data represented by its inputs – the incoming solid arrows – into an output value, according to some specified *decision logic*. The most common form of decision logic is a decision table.

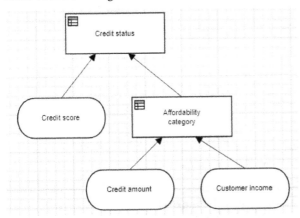

Figure 5-3. DRD for *Credit status*

For example, the decision *Credit status* depends on the values of the inputs *Credit score* and *Affordability category*. *Affordability category* is itself a decision, based on the inputs *Credit amount* and *Customer income*. DRDs allow you to break down complex decision logic into a tree of simpler supporting decisions.

	Affordability category	Credit score	Credit status
P	tAffordabilityCategory Affordable, Marginal, Unaffordable	Number	tCreditStatus Credit ok, Bad credit
1	"Affordable"	>620	"Credit ok"
2	"Marginal"	>680	"Credit ok"
3	-	-	"Bad credit"

Figure 5-4. Decision table for *Credit status*

Figure 5-4 illustrates the decision logic for *Credit Status*, a decision table. Its allowed values, shown in the output column heading, are *Credit ok* or *Bad credit*. The input *Affordability category* has allowed values *Affordable, Marginal,* or *Unaffordable,* and the input *Credit score* is a number.

Each row in the table is a rule. The table says if *Affordability category* is *Affordable* and *Credit score* is greater than 620, then *Credit status* is *Credit ok;* if *Affordability category* is *Marginal* and *Credit score* is greater than 680, then *Credit status* is *Credit ok;* otherwise, *Credit status* is *Bad credit.* A separate decision table defines the logic determining *Affordability category* from the inputs *Credit amount* and *Customer income.*

DMN supports other decision logic types beside decision tables and a rich expression language called FEEL, but for simple routing decisions all you need to know are DRDs and basic decision tables.

Integrating BPMN and DMN

Method and Style provides a simple procedure for transforming Bad BPMN like Figure 5-1 into Good BPMN. Here is how it works.

Following *Method and Style,* we want to create a decision task with one end state per next step in the process. Each end state is a distinct output value of the DMN decision table. The gateways in the original BPMN give us the input data and rules.

Let's start with the first chain of gateways, to be replaced by the decision task *Routing 1* (Figure 5-5). Following the decision there are 3 possible next steps: the process end event *Denied,* the task *Adjudicate claim,* and the task *Determine risk category.* So our decision output has 3 allowed output values, one per next step. I called mine *Denied, Adjudicate,* and *Autopay.*

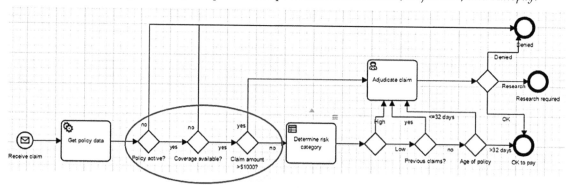

Figure 5-5. Gateway chain to be replaced by DMN decision *Routing 1*

The gateways tell us the input data elements we need for the decision. They are:

- *is Policy Active* (boolean)
- *is Coverage Available* (boolean)
- *Claim Amount* (number)

The resulting DRD is shown in Figure 5-6.

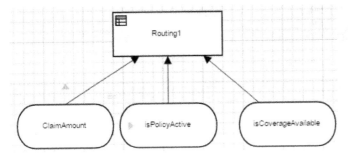

Figure 5-6. DRD for *Routing 1*

The rules of the decision table are given by the original process model, following the paths out of the gateways (Figure 5-7).

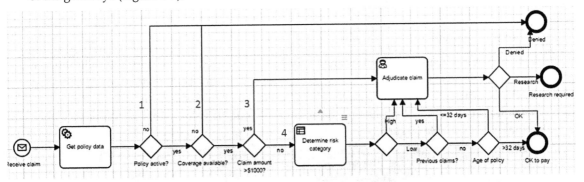

Figure 5-7. Outgoing sequence flows determine the rules

1. If *is Policy Active* = false then *Denied*

2. If *is Policy Active* = true and *is Coverage Available* = false then *Denied*

3. If *is Policy Active* = true and *is Coverage Available* = true and *Claim Amount* >1000 then *Adjudicate*

4. If *is Policy Active* = true and *is Coverage Available* = true and *Claim Amount* <=1000 then *Autopay*

The resulting decision table is shown in Figure 5-8. Each row in the table matches the corresponding rule listed here.

U	is Policy Active	is Coverage Available	Claim amount	Routing1
	Boolean true, false	Boolean true, false	Number	Text [Denied, Adjudicate, Autopay]
1	false	-	-	"Denied"
2	true	false	-	"Denied"
3	true	true	>1000	"Adjudicate"
4	true	true	<=1000	"Autopay"

Figure 5-8. Decision table for _Routing 1_

A hyphen in a decision table cell means that input is irrelevant in the rule. The code _U_ in the top left corner, called the table's _hit policy_, means that any combination of input values matches exactly one rule. Alternatively, hit policy _A_ allows some input combinations to match multiple rules as long as they have the same output value. This sometimes allows a simpler decision table (Figure 5-9).

A	is Policy Active	is Coverage Available	Claim Amount	Routing1
	Boolean	Boolean	Number	tRouting1 ["Denied", "Adjudicate", "Autopay"]
1	false	-	-	"Denied"
2	-	false	-	"Denied"
3	true	true	>1000	"Adjudicate"
4	true	true	<=1000	"Autopay"

Figure 5-9. Hit policy A table for _Routing 1_

We can do the same thing for the second chain of gateways, to be replaced by _Routing 2_. Following a similar procedure, the decision table for that looks like Figure 5-10 in a _U_ table or Figure 5-11 in the simpler _A_ table.

	Risk Category	has Previous Claims	Age Days	Routing2
U	Text [High, Low]	Boolean true, false	Number	Text [OK, Adjudicate]
1	"High"	-	-	"Adjudicate"
2	"Low"	true	-	"Adjudicate"
3	"Low"	false	<=32	"Adjudicate"
4	"Low"	false	>32	"OK"

Figure 5-10. Decision table for *Routing 2*

	Risk Category	has Previous Claims	Age Days	Routing2
A	Text [High, Low]	Boolean true, false	Number	Text [OK, Adjudicate]
1	"High"	-	-	"Adjudicate"
2	-	true	-	"Adjudicate"
3	-	-	<=32	"Adjudicate"
4	"Low"	false	>32	"OK"

Figure 5-11. Hit policy A table for *Routing 2*

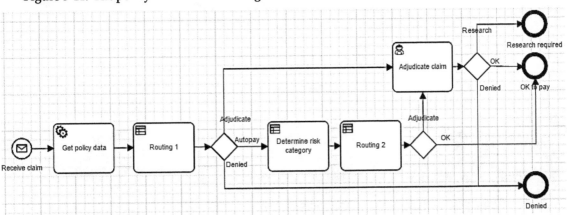

Figure 5-12. Good BPMN using *Routing 1* and *Routing 2*

The resulting Good BPMN model is shown in Figure 5-12. The decision tasks *Routing 1* and *Routing 2* invoke the DMN decisions of the same name. Each decision output value corresponds to an end state of the decision task, and thus to a gate of the gateway that leads to the next step. Following this simple procedure makes it easy to turn any chain of gateways into Good BPMN. For more information on decision modeling with DMN, I refer you to my book *DMN Method and Style*[13] and my DMN Basics[14] and DMN Advanced[15] training.

---

[13] https://www.amazon.com/dp/0982368151

[14] https://methodandstyle.com/product/dmn-basics-on-demand/

[15] https://methodandstyle.com/product/dmn-advanced-on-demand/

CHAPTER 6

Parallel Flow

Parallel flow refers to paths in the process model that run concurrently. We've already seen the Parallel (AND) gateway, which unconditionally – i.e., in every process instance – splits the instance into two or more parallel paths or joins those paths into one. BPMN also defines another type of gateway representing *conditionally parallel flow*, and that is the focus of this chapter.

Conditionally Parallel Flow

The *inclusive gateway*, also called the *OR gateway*, with the O symbol inside, represents *conditional split*. This means that under some conditions – in some process instances – the flow out of the gateway includes parallel paths. Like the XOR gateway, each gate has a Boolean condition, but here the conditions are *independent*. More than one of them could be true at the same time, and each gate with a true condition is enabled. If two or more are enabled, those paths run in parallel. Unlike XOR gateway, an OR gateway is not required to follow an activity and test its end state.

Figure 6-1 illustrates a bank deposit reporting process. If it is a cash deposit over $10,000, perform large cash deposit reporting. If it is a deposit in foreign currency, perform foreign currency deposit reporting. Those conditions are independent; they could both be true at the same time, and in that case, both gates of the OR gateway are enabled in parallel. So this represents conditionally parallel – i.e., possibly parallel – flow.

In the left diagram of Figure 6-1, one gate has a slash or tickmark and no label. This is called the *default gate*. Default here means "otherwise". It means enable this gate only if no other gate has a true condtion. Default is *not* the same as always. If you mean always enable this gate and under certain conditions enable the other gates, label the gate "always", as in the diagram on the right. These two diagrams do not mean the same thing.

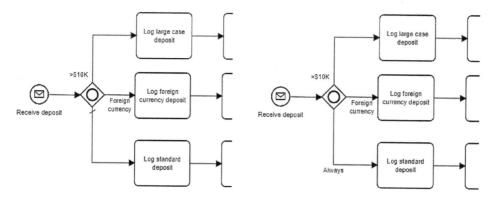

Figure 6-1. Conditional split using OR gateway. Default means *otherwise*, not *always*

Merging Alternative Paths

Proper merging of sequence flows depends on whether the flows are exclusive alternatives, unconditionally parallel, or conditionally parallel.

If the paths to be merged represent *exclusive alternatives*, just merge them directly (Figure 6-2, left). In order to tell if they are exclusive alternatives, you need to look upstream to see how they were split in the first place. If they were split by an XOR gateway, they are by definition exclusive alternatives.

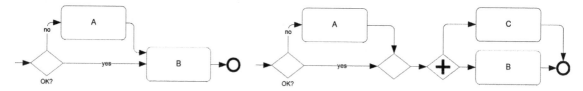

Figure 6-2. Merge alternative paths directly into an activity. You may use XOR gateway to merge into another gateway.

An XOR gateway used as a merge is the same as no gateway at all. It simply passes through each incoming sequence flow as it arrives. For merging alternative paths into an activity it is completely redundant, so best to omit it. However, you may want to use it to merge alternative paths into another gateway (Figure 6-2, right), since the behavior of a gateway with multiple inputs and multiple outputs is ambiguous. A style rule says a gateway should be explicitly branching or merging.

Merging Parallel Paths

If paths are parallel or conditionally parallel, you may not merge them directly or with XOR gateway (Figure 6-3). That is called *multi-merge,* and it means the node following the merge is triggered twice (and nodes downstream as well). In Method and Style, multi-merge is not allowed. Instead you must use a *join*. The proper gateway to use at the join depends on whether the incoming flows are unconditionally or conditionally parallel.

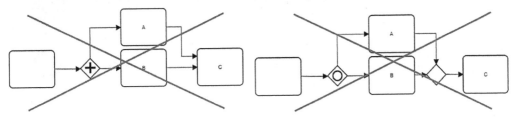

Figure 6-3. Merging parallel or conditionally parallel flow without a join is multi-merge, an error

AND Gateway Join

If paths are *unconditionally parallel*, split by an AND gateway, use an AND gateway to join them. For example (Figure 6-4), *Draft contract*, then in parallel *Perform legal review* and *Perform financial review*. An AND gateway join waits for *all* incoming sequence flows to arrive before continuing. This means *Finalize contract* may not start until both the legal review and financial review are complete.

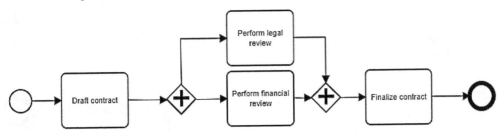

Figure 6-4. To join parallel paths into an activity, use AND gateway

Now suppose we make a slight modification: If the legal review finds a compliance issue, we branch to *Modify for compliance* before *Finalize contract*. Now the AND join is incorrect (Figure 6-5). The problem is that the AND gateway join always waits for all its inputs. There are three of them, but in any instance only two will arrive, so this join is *deadlocked*.

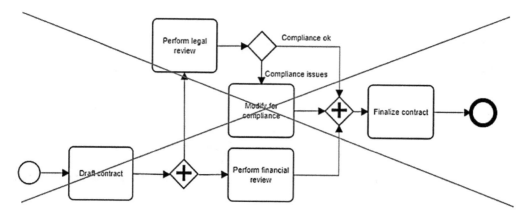

Figure 6-5. Conditionally parallel inputs create a deadlock at AND join

OR Gateway Join

The way to resolve the deadlock is with an OR gateway join (Figure 6-6). An OR gateway join waits for all incoming sequence flows that are enabled in this instance. It does not wait for inputs that will never arrive.

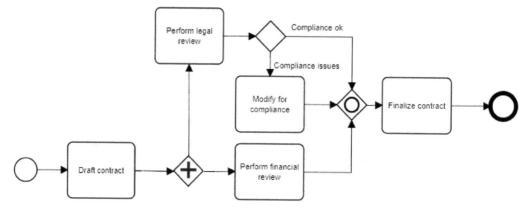

Figure 6-6. OR gateway join merges conditionally parallel flows

Which inputs those are is not knowable when this process starts, but as soon as *Perform legal review* is complete it is knowable whether the *Compliance ok* or *Compliance issues* gate is enabled.

The general rule is this:

> *Use OR gateway join whenever:*

1. There is the possibility that *at least two* incoming sequence flows are parallel, and…

2. We cannot guarantee that *all* incoming sequence flows are enabled in this instance

Our bank deposit reporting process is another example of conditionally parallel flow, requiring an OR gateway join (Figure 6-7).

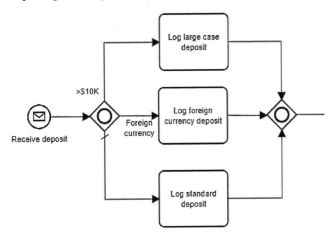

Figure 6-7. Another example of OR gateway join

CHAPTER 7

Events

The BPMN spec defines an event as "something that happens" in a process. It would be more accurate to say that a BPMN event describes *how the process responds to a signal that something happened*, or – in the case of a throwing event – *how the process generates a signal that something happened*. The type of signal, called the *trigger* for catching events and the *result* for throwing events, is indicated by the icon inside the circle.

The spec defines 13 trigger/result types and 8 behavior types, including start events, end events, and 6 others. Of the resulting 104 combinations, approximately half are not allowed (Figure 7-1). This is way too complicated.

Fortunately, very few of these are used in practice. We will focus on the Big 3, the ones you need to know: Timer, Message, and Error events. The others you can safely ignore.

Intermediate Events

Intermediate events (Figure 7-1) occur after the start and before the end of a process level. They all have a double ring shape, but what makes intermediate events tricky is that they describe several different process behaviors, distinguished by only small differences in how the event is drawn.

- A *throwing* intermediate event, with the black icon inside, means the process *generates* the trigger signal. Of the Big 3, only Message supports the throwing behavior. By convention, throwing the signal occurs immediately and automatically as soon as the incoming sequence flow arrives, and the process continues immediately afterward on the sequence flow out of the throwing event.

- A *catching* intermediate event, with the white icon inside, drawn with sequence flow in and sequence flow out, means the process *waits* for the trigger signal. When the trigger signal arrives, the process resumes on the sequence flow out of the event. Of the Big 3, Message and Timer support catching behavior, but not Error.

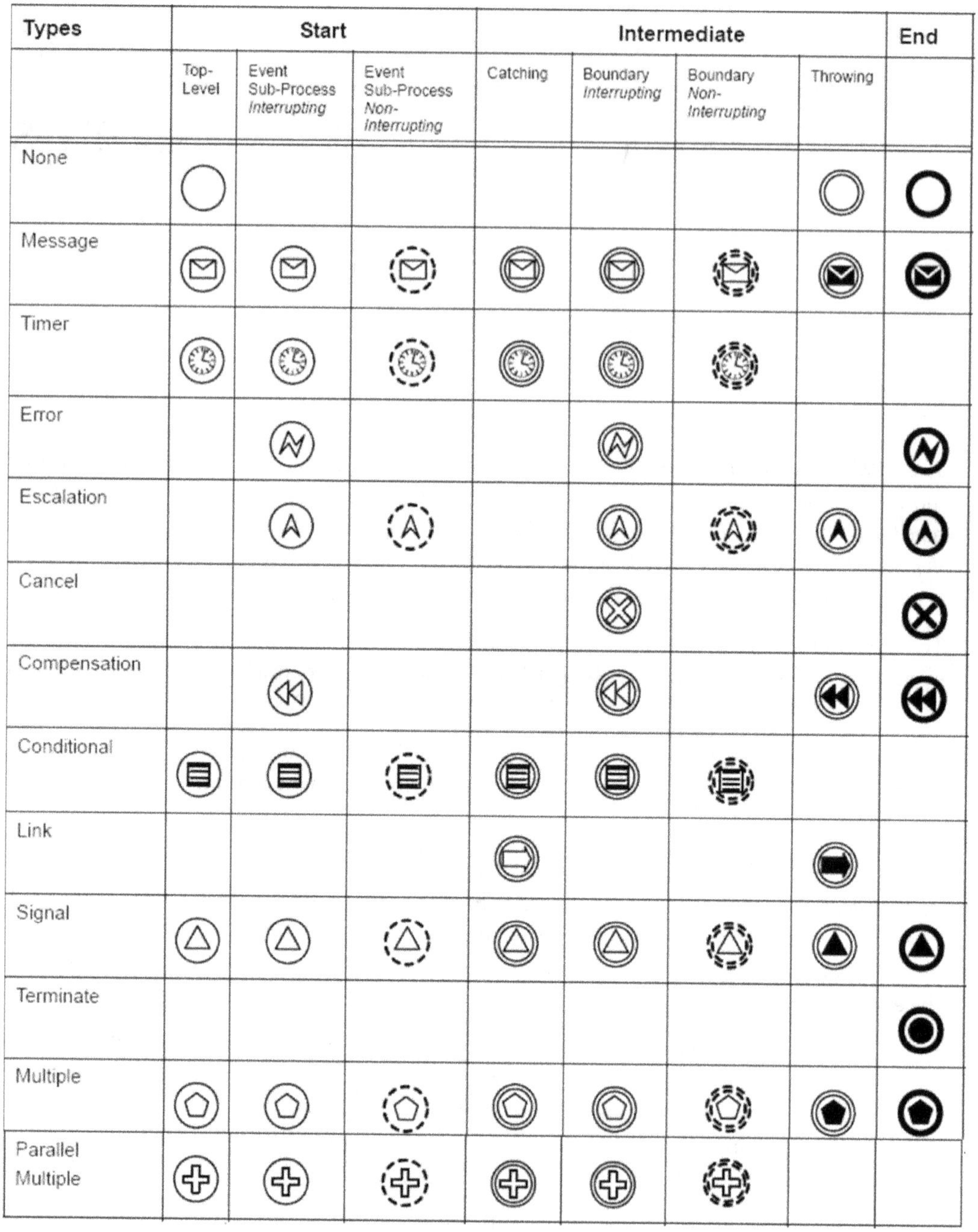

Types	Start			Intermediate				End
	Top-Level	Event Sub-Process *Interrupting*	Event Sub-Process *Non-Interrupting*	Catching	Boundary *Interrupting*	Boundary *Non-Interrupting*	Throwing	
None	◯						◯	◯
Message	✉	✉	✉	✉	✉	✉	✉	✉
Timer	⏲	⏲	⏲	⏲	⏲	⏲		
Error		⃠			⃠			⃠
Escalation		Ⓐ	Ⓐ		Ⓐ	Ⓐ	Ⓐ	Ⓐ
Cancel					⊗			⊗
Compensation		◀◀			◀◀		◀◀	◀◀
Conditional	▤	▤	▤	▤	▤	▤		
Link				▭			▭	
Signal	△	△	△	△	△	△	▲	▲
Terminate								⬤
Multiple	⬠	⬠	⬠	⬠	⬠	⬠	⬠	⬠
Parallel Multiple	✛	✛	✛	✛	✛	✛		

Figure 7-1. BPMN 2.0 events – full element set

Figure 7-2 Catching (left) and throwing (right) Message event

- An intermediate event with white icon attached to the boundary of an activity, is called a *boundary event*. It does not signify waiting. It means while the activity is running, the process *listens* for that signal. If it occurs before the activity completes, the sequence flow out of the event, called the *exception flow*, is triggered. On the other hand, if the activity completes without the occurrence of the boundary event signal, the exception flow is ignored and the process continues on the sequence flow out of the activity, called the *normal flow*.

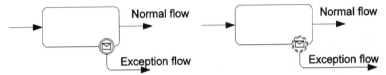

Figure 7-3. Interrupting (left) and non-interrupting (right) Message boundary event

A boundary event has no incoming sequence flow and must have *exactly one* outgoing sequence flow, the exception flow. There are two types of boundary event. An *interrupting boundary event*, denoted by the solid double ring, means the activity that the event is attached to is terminated immediately upon occurrence of the trigger signal. The process does not exit on the normal flow but continues immediately on the exception flow, the sequence flow out of the event. With interrupting boundary events, the exception flow and normal flow represent alternative paths. Message, Timer, and Error events all support interrupting boundary event behavior.

A *non-interrupting boundary event*, denoted by the dashed double ring, does not terminate the activity. That activity continues uninterrupted, and when it completes, the process continues on the normal flow, the sequence flow out of the activity. But, in addition, upon occurrence of the trigger a new parallel path of the process is instantiated immediately on the exception flow. In this case, the exception flow represents actions taken *in addition* to those on the normal flow, so the exception flow and normal flow represent conditionally parallel paths. Message and Timer events support non-interrupting boundary event behavior, but Error boundary events are always interrupting.

Timer Event

Catching Timer Event

Drawn with sequence flow in and out, a catching Timer intermediate event represents a *delay*. It means either *wait for [specified duration]* or *wait until [specified date/time]*. For example, you might want to wait for a short while before retrying an activity such as polling for posted data (Figure 7-4, top). You can also use a catching Timer event to model a wait for a scheduled action, such as a semi-monthly check run (Figure 7-4, bottom).

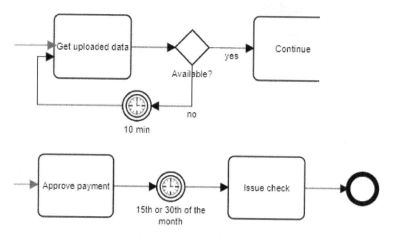

Figure 7-4. Delay using catching Timer event

A catching Timer event does NOT mean wait for something to occur, such as a response to a request; that would be a Message event. And you don't use a catching Timer event to signify that an activity "usually" takes three days; you would use a Timer boundary event to say *what happens if the activity takes longer* than three days.

Timer Boundary Event

The more common use of a Timer event is as boundary event, where it signifies *deadline-triggered action*. If an activity is not complete by its deadline, do something immediately at the deadline. The deadline is specified by the event label, either a duration measured from the arrival of the sequence flow at the activity or a specific date and time. If the activity is not complete by the deadline, the event is triggered. Remember, BPMN does not have a way to say how long something *usually* takes, but it does let you say what happens if it takes too long to complete.

What happens then depends on whether the event is interrupting or non-interrupting. An *interrupting Timer event*, with the solid double ring, aborts the activity at the deadline and exits immediately on the exception flow.

For example (Figure 7-5), you could use an interrupting Timer event in a hiring process to indicate that if a search for internal candidates does not complete within two weeks, you want to abandon it and engage an external search firm. Note that because the exception flow and normal flow are exclusive alternatives, they can be merged at *Screen applicants* without a gateway.

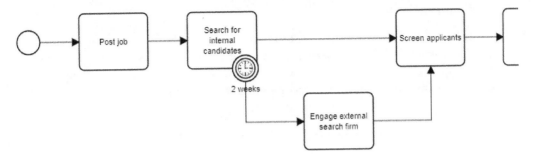

Figure 7-5. Interrupting Timer boundary event

A *non-interrupting Timer event,* with the dashed double ring, immediately initiates the exception flow without aborting the activity or the normal flow out of it. If something takes too long, you often want to keep doing it but do something else in addition, such as notify the requester, notify the manager, or get additional help.

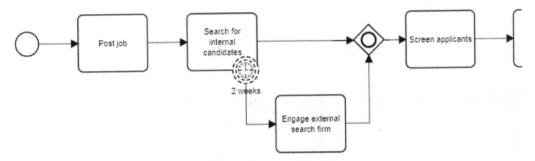

Figure 7-6. Non-interrupting Timer boundary event

For example (Figure 7-6), suppose we want to engage the external search firm if our internal search is not complete in two weeks, but we don't want to terminate the internal search. That would use the non-interrupting Timer boundary event. If the exception flow is triggered, we have parallel flow. *Engage external search firm* and *Search for internal candidates* are running concurrently. This is conditionally parallel flow, because it occurs only when the internal search exceeds the deadline. That means when we merge the exception flow downstream with the normal flow, we need an OR gateway join.

Make a note of this: With non-interrupting events, you always use an OR gateway join to merge the exception flow with the normal flow downstream.

Since it does not abort the activity it is attached to, a non-interrupting Timer event could be triggered multiple times. For example, you could send a reminder or notification on the exception flow every hour until the activity is complete. In that case, label the event *Every hour.*

Timed Interval

A Timer boundary event measures the time from start to completion of a *single activity*, but what if you want to time the interval from point A to point B in the process, spanning *multiple activities*? That's easy. Just wrap the fragment from point A to point B in a *subprocess*, and attach the Timer event to the subprocess boundary.

Figure 7-7 illustrates a fast food process: Take the order, collect the money, in parallel prepare the burger, fries, and drink, and when all those are complete deliver to the customer.

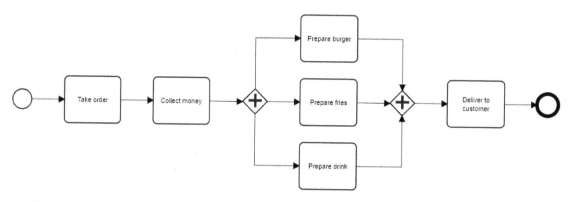

Figure 7-7. To time an interval spanning multiple activities...

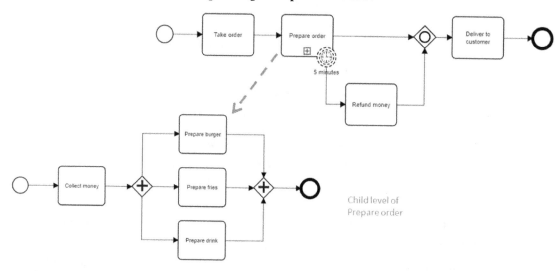

Child level of
Prepare order

Figure 7-8. ...wrap the interval in a subprocess and attach Timer boundary event.

Now we'd like to say if the order isn't ready to deliver to the customer within 5 minutes of taking the order, the restaurant will refund the money. In other words we want to time an interval spanning multiple activities, as shown in Figure 7-7 . We can do that by enclosing that interval in a subprocess, and attaching a non-interrupting Timer event to it (Figure 7-8).

Putting these ideas all together, here is an exercise on Timer events we do in our BPMN Method and Style training. The scenario goes like this:

> Upon receipt of a support request, assess the problem (and assign it to a tech), fix the problem, verify with the customer, and end. If fixing the problem is not complete within 1 hour of receiving the request, notify the customer with the expected completion time.

The solution is shown in Figure 7-9. Because the timed interval starts upon receipt of the message and ends upon completion of Fix the problem, we need to attach the Timer event to a subprocess enclosing both *Assess the problem* and *Fix the problem*. This is a very common pattern with boundary events.

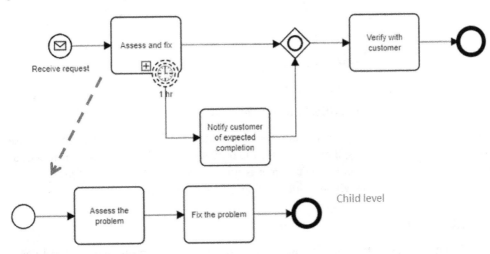

Figure 7-9. Diagram of the timed interval scenario

Timer Event vs. Gateway

Beginners sometimes try to test the duration of an activity using a gateway following the activity. That is incorrect, because the process does not arrive at the gateway until *after* the activity finishes, and by then the triggered action is too late. The whole point of a boundary event is that its action occurs *immediately* upon the timeout, *before* the activity it is attached to is complete. Here is an illustration.

Consider the two diagrams in Figure 7-10, intended to show notifying the customer if *Perform service* takes longer than one hour. The question is this: Does the customer notification occur at the same time in both diagrams?

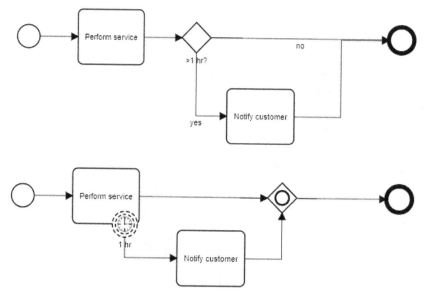

Figure 7-10. Does customer notification occur at same time in both diagrams?

The answer is *No*. With the gateway, the customer is not notified until *after Perform Service completes*, no matter how long that takes. That is probably not what the modeler intended. With the Timer boundary event, the customer is notified *after exactly 1 hour* if the activity is not yet complete. That's the whole point of using a Timer boundary event.

Message Event

Before diving into the details of Message events, we need to say more about what BPMN means by "sending" and "receiving."

Message and Message Flow

The terms *send* and *receive* should be considered keywords in BPMN, reserved specifically for sending and receiving a *message*, represented in the diagram by a *message flow*. In BPMN a "message" means any communication between the process and an outside entity – a customer or service provider, another internal process, or possibly even an IT system. The BPMN 2.0 specification defines a message as simply "the content of a communication between two participants." That communication could take any form. It does not have to be a system-to-system message, as it would be in an executable process. In non-executable process models it is more likely some form of human communications, such as a letter, fax, email or phone call. We use message to mean any one-way communication between a process element and something outside the process.

Send Task and Throwing Message Event

The term *send* in BPMN implies sending a message, and thus a message flow. A message may be sent from a black-box pool, a throwing Message event, or an activity.

A *send task* (Figure 7-11, left), with the black envelope icon, is a task that simply sends a message immediately and exits. Sending the message is all that it does. Style rules require drawing a message flow attached to a Send task.

Figure 7-11. Send task and throwing Message intermediate event

Alternatively, a *throwing Message intermediate event* (Figure 7-11, right) does the same thing. Effectively it is the same as a send task. When the incoming sequence flow arrives, it sends a message and then immediately continues. You might ask why BPMN has two different elements that do exactly the same thing. Good question. I don't know.

Actually, there is a small difference between a throwing Message event and a send task. As a type of activity, a send task has a *performer*; the message is sent by an actor in the process. A throwing Message event means the message is sent by "the process", such as the process engine in an automated process. This is a distinction that makes sense only in automated processes. Also, you can attach a marker to a send task to signify that it is performed multiple times, i.e., sends multiple messages; you cannot do that with an event. But for all practical purposes they are identical.

"Sending" Within a Process

A common beginner mistake is to use a send task to forward work to a downstream task (Figure 7-12). Since the "sender" and "receiver" are part of the same process, you may not use a message. Thus a send task is incorrect. In fact, since "send" is a sort of BPMN keyword, you should not even use the word "send" in the label of a user task!

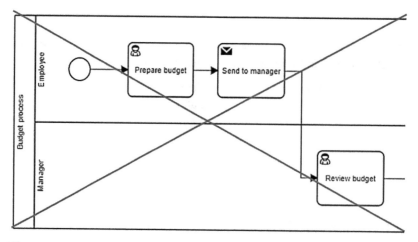

Figure 7-12. Don't use a send task to communicate within a process

So how do you "send" work to a downstream task performer, or simply notify a Manager in another lane of the process? In the case of forwarding work downstream, usually the best choice is not to model the "sending" action explicitly at all. It is simply *implied* by the sequence flow (Figure 7-13).

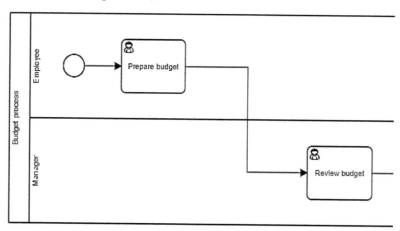

Figure 7-13. "Sending" work downstream is implied by sequence flow alone

It could be, however, that forwarding the budget materials to the Manager is not just attaching a spreadsheet to an email. Let's say it requires packing up two drawers of a file cabinet and carting it off to Fedex. And let's say that effort is exactly the kind of thing you want to improve upon in the to-be process, so you don't want to hide it inside a sequence flow. In such a case, you should make it a task, but a user task not a send task (Figure 7-14). Since there is no BPMN message involved, don't even use the verb "Send" in the label. Instead use names like *Pack and Ship*.

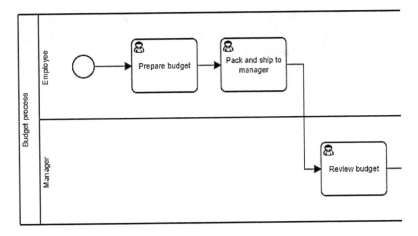

Figure 7-14. User task can represent the work of "sending" within a process

Receive Task and Catching Message Event

Receiving is closely related to sending. Again, the term technically applies only to messages, communications from external participants. We have already seen that a Message start event creates a new process instance when the message is received, but we can also receive a message in the middle of a process.

A *receive task*, with the white envelope icon (Figure 7-15, left), *waits for a message*. That is the only thing it does. When the incoming sequence flow arrives, the process instance pauses; when the message flow arrives, the process immediately resumes on the outgoing sequence flow.

Figure 7-15. Receive task and catching Message intermediate event

A *catching Message intermediate event* (Figure 7-15, right), drawn with sequence flow in and out, has the same meaning as a receive task. It waits for a message, and immediately exits when the message is received. As with sending, there is a tiny difference between a receive task and a catching Message event. You can attach a Timer boundary event to a receive task, but you cannot do that with a Message event. As it turns out, there is another way to accomplish the same thing, and we'll see that shortly.

Event Gateway

Figure 7-16 illustrates use of throwing and catching Message intermediate events in a process for issuing a credit card. If the Customer's application is missing required information, the process sends a request for it and waits for the response. Whenever you use a Message event you should draw the message flow, and label both the event and the message flow. The event should be labeled with the action – *Request X*, for example – and the message flow should be labeled with the name of the message.

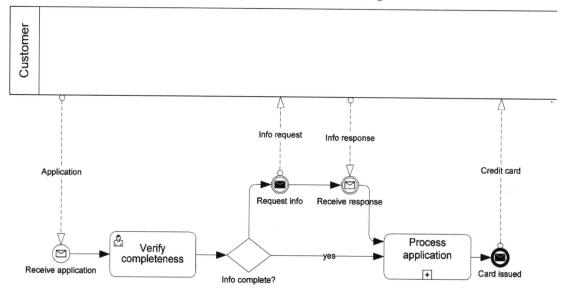

Figure 7-16. Throwing and catching Message intermediate events

When there is a possibility that the response may not be returned before some deadline, you should not wait for it using a "naked" Message event as in Figure 7-16. If the customer decides not to respond to the request, the process instance will wait forever at the catching Message event. Real processes don't work that way. They will wait up to some maximum time, and then do something else. You can model that behavior with a Timer boundary event on a receive task, but there is a way to do the same thing with a catching Message event.

Figure 7-17 is a better way to wait for the response message. It's called an *event gateway*. The symbol inside the gateway shape is the *Multiple intermediate event*, and on each gate there is a catching intermediate event, usually a Message event and a Timer event.

Like the regular XOR gateway, an event gateway represents an exclusive choice – i.e., only one of the gates is enabled – but the choice is not based on a process data condition. The gate that is enabled is the event that occurs *first*. An event gateway may have two or more gates, each representing an event, and it's a race between them. In Figure 7-17 it's a race between the response message and a timeout. If the *Info response* message is received within 7 days, the Message event gate is enabled and the instance continues to *Process application*. If it is not received in 7 days, the Timer event gate is enabled and the instance continues to the *Rejected* end state.

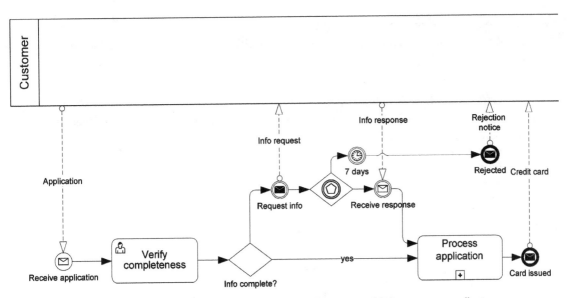

Figure 7-17. Event gateway waits for response or timeout, whichever occurs first

Message Boundary Event

A message you are paused waiting for usually implies a response to a prior request. But BPMN provides a way to respond to *unsolicited messages* as well. In that case, the process is not paused waiting for the message, but listening for it while running. A *Message boundary event* attached to an activity initiates the response to the message if it arrives while the activity is running. An *interrupting boundary event* aborts the activity immediately upon receipt of the message and exits on the *exception flow*, the sequence flow out of the event. Upon receipt of the message, a *non-interrupting boundary event* continues the activity but immediately initiates a parallel action on the exception flow. If the activity completes without the message arriving, the exception flow is not triggered. The process simply continues on the *normal flow*, the sequence flow out of the activity.

Figure 7-18. Interrupting (left) and non-interrupting (right) Message boundary events

For example, if the customer cancels an order while it is being fulfilled (Figure 7-18, left), an interrupting Message boundary event immediately terminates *Fulfill Order* and exits on the exception flow. On the other hand, if the customer updates shipping information while the order is being fulfilled (Figure 7-18, right), you do not want to terminate *Fulfill Order* but initiate something else in addition, such as adding the updated shipping information to the order. The exception-triggered action is on the exception flow. When *Fulfill Order* completes, processing continues on the normal flow. With non-interrupting events, the normal flow and exception flow exits represent conditionally parallel paths, so they must be merged using an OR gateway join.

Quite often, a single physical message is represented in the process model by multiple message flows, each leading to a different Message boundary event. Suppose the Customer cancels an order while it is being processed. How is that handled? The answer is, "It depends..." How cancellation is handled immediately after the order is placed may not be the same as when it is ready to ship.

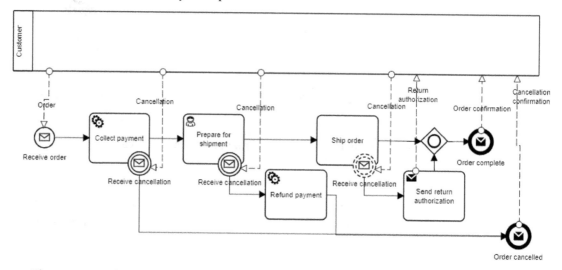

Figure 7-19. One physical message modeled as multiple message flows to separate boundary events

For example, in Figure 7-19 we see that the message *Cancellation* aborts the order process and returns a *Cancellation confirmation* message if it is received during *Collect payment* or *Prepare for shipment*. However, if the same message is received during *Ship order*, the process in this case is not terminated. A new action, *Send return authorization* is triggered, but *Ship order* continues, and when it finishes the process goes to *Order complete*. Both the exception flow and normal flow are enabled in this case, requiring the OR gateway join.

Alternative Triggers

Before leaving message events, we should mention that although most processes have a single start event, it is possible to have more than one. Typically these are Message start events, each representing an *alternative trigger* for the process. The most common use case for this is multiple channels to the requester, with a different initial step for each channel. For example, an order could come in through the web or the call center, with order entry specific to the channel but sharing a common fulfillment and billing (Figure 7-20). The triggers are alternatives, not parallel, so the flows are merged downstream without a join.

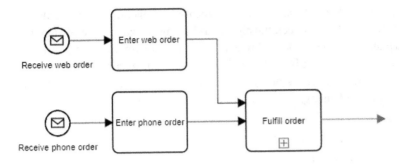

Figure 7-20. Alternative process triggers

Error Event

The last of the Big 3 event types is the *Error event*. The only Error intermediate event that exists is an interrupting boundary event, meaning the activity it's attached to ended in the exception end state named by the event label. In that case, the process exits on the exception flow. The normal flow exit thus represents ending in *not* that exception end state.

An Error event on the boundary of a task simply represents the *exception end state exit* from the task. The normal flow, the sequence flow out of the task, represents the exit when the task completes successfully. The behavior is exactly the same as an XOR gateway following the task with a success gate and an exception gate (Figure 7-21).

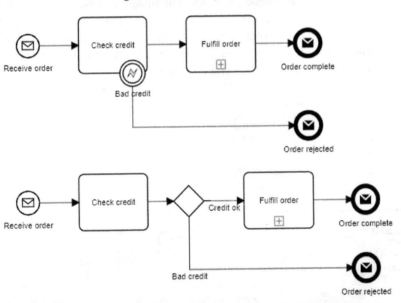

Figure 7-21. An Error boundary event on a task is equivalent to testing the task end state with a gateway

In the first edition of *BPMN Method and Style*, I advocated reserving Error events for *technical exceptions*, such as inability to check the credit, and using the gateway end state test to handle *business exceptions* like *Bad credit*. However, based on feedback from students I later revised that advice. Now I say it is perfectly fine to use Error events for any type of exception, business or technical. There is no implied semantic distinction between testing the end state in a gateway and using an Error event, although you could adopt such a convention for your organization.

What if the task *Check credit* in Figure 7-21 were a *subprocess* instead? As before, the boundary event *Bad credit* signifies that the activity has an exception end state *Bad credit*. But, unlike a task, a subprocess exposes its end states explicitly via its end events. So a *Bad credit* Error boundary event on a subprocess implies the child-level expansion must contain an end event called *Bad credit*. This is not just Method and Style; this is from the BPMN spec. Not only must there be a *Bad credit* end event in the child-level expansion, but it must be an *Error end event*.

An Error end event in a subprocess throws an error signal to the boundary of the subprocess, where it is caught by the Error boundary event and exits on the exception flow. This is called the *Error throw-catch pattern*. You could think of it as *propagating an exception from child to parent levels* in the model.

This is illustrated in Figure 7-22. The *Bad credit* error is thrown from a child-level end event to a boundary event at the parent level. In the BPMN metamodel, both the Error end event and Error boundary event reference the same *error code*, but since the error code does not appear in the diagram, Method and Style says the event *labels* of the error thrower and catcher must match. Following some exception handling at the child level (*Update customer info*), the error throw-catch propagates the exception to the parent level for additional exception handling at that level (*Contact customer* and end the process).

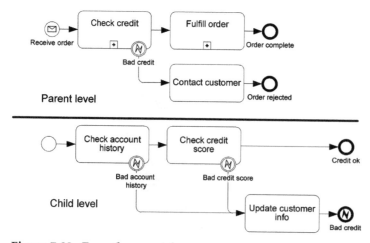

Figure 7-22. Error throw-catch

Thus Error events are really just a notational convenience, since we can describe the same behavior with gateways. Figure 7-23, the gateway end state test from Level 1, means exactly the same thing as Figure 7-22, using Error throw-catch. The gateway end state test also propagates exceptions from child level to parent level.

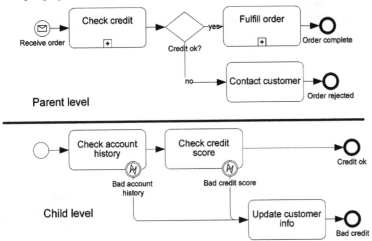

Figure 7-23. Gateway end state test

In the examples presented so far, the error is thrown when the child level is already complete, so the "interrupting" Error boundary event doesn't really interrupt anything – the subprocess is already over. But it is possible that the child-level expansion has parallel paths reaching separate end events. If one of them is an Error end event, then throwing the error terminates the subprocess even if the other path has not yet reached its end event. With parallel paths, Error throw-catch acts like the gateway end state test where the exception end state is a Terminate, not a None end event.

With Error events, we now need to modify slightly one of the basic style rules we have been using. Previously we said that the count of gates on an XOR gateway must equal the count of end states of the previous activity. But the actual rule is this:

> **The count of gates on an XOR gateway must equal the count of *non-Error end states* of the previous activity.**

Error end states have their own exit from the activity – the exception flow – so they are not tested by a gateway.

Event Subprocess

There is one additional form of event-triggered action that is not so well known. Until recently, I even omitted it from my training, but now I find it is useful enough to warrant inclusion. It's called an *event subprocess*, a special kind of subprocess that is triggered by an event. Regular subprocesses, you remember, are triggered by incoming sequence flow.

They must have a None start event. Event subprocesses are different: They have no incoming sequence flow and they must have a triggered start event.

Interrupting Message Event Subprocess

An event subprocess is an alternative to boundary events. A boundary event handles an event trigger occurring during a particular activity. An event subprocess handles an event trigger occurring *at any time in the entire process level*. In Figure 7-24, *Handle customer cancel* is an event subprocess. Like all event subprocesses, it has a dotted border, no incoming or outgoing sequence flow, and a trigger icon in the top left corner. The trigger icon looks like a start event. It could be either interrupting – solid single ring – or non-interrupting – dashed single ring.

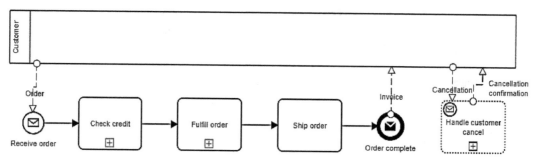

Figure 7-24. Event subprocess in a top process level

Here the event subprocess is floating in the top process level, meaning if the trigger – the *Cancellation* message – occurs any time during the entire process, terminate the regular process and run the event subprocess. So while boundary events define separate handlers at each activity in the process level, an event subprocess defines a *single event handler applicable everywhere in the process level*.

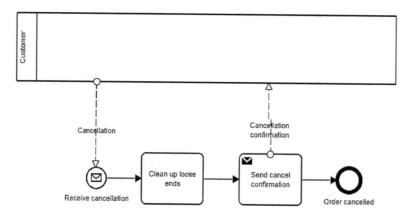

Figure 7-25. Child level of event subprocess

The child level of *Handle customer cancel* is shown in Figure 7-25. It has an interrupting Message start event, which is replicated in the parent level diagram Figure 7-24. It sends a *Cancellation confirmation* message, also replicated. The event subprocess end event *Order cancelled* defines a second end state for the process.

Non-Interrupting Timer Event Subprocess

A Timer event subprocess tests the duration of an entire process level. If the regular process level is not complete by the deadline, the event subprocess is triggered.

Previously in this chapter we saw how a Timer boundary event is used to put a deadline on a process fragment. That diagram is reproduced in Figure 7-26.

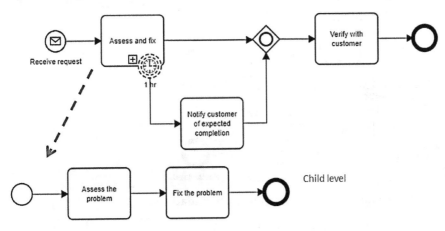

Figure 7-26. Deadline handling using non-interrupting boundary event

But we can do something equivalent using an event subprocess (Figure 7-27). Instead of a boundary event on *Assess and fix* in the parent level, we have a Timer event subprocess *Notify customer* floating in the child level of *Assess and fix*. Here we use the inline expansion of *Notify customer*, with the expanded subprocess shape, in order to visualize the details of *Notify customer* in the same diagram as the regular subprocess *Assess and fix*.

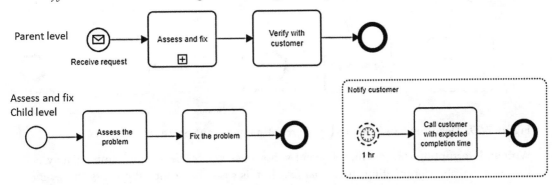

Figure 7-27. Deadline handling using non-interrupting event subprocess

Notice that the start event has the dashed border, meaning non-interrupting. Like a boundary event, a non-interrupting event subprocess start event means initiate the event subprocess immediately upon the trigger but don't terminate the regular subprocess. They both run concurrently. The process level is not complete until both the regular subprocess and event subprocess are complete, at which point control returns to the parent level process. The behavior of Figure 7-26 and Figure 7-27 is identical.

Interrupting Timer Event Subprocess

Here is one final wrinkle on the previous example. Suppose if *Assess and fix* takes longer than 1 hour we don't notify the customer and continue, but instead reschedule the fix and end the process. Using a Timer boundary event it looks like Figure 7-28, but we could alternatively use an interrupting Timer event subprocess (Figure 7-29).

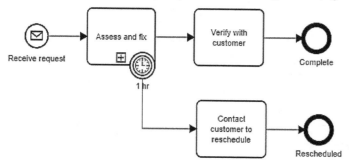

Figure 7-28. Deadline handling using interrupting boundary event

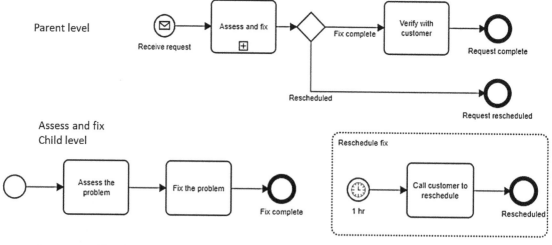

Figure 7-29. Deadline handling using interrupting event subprocess

With an interrupting start event, the event subprocess *Reschedule fix* starts immediately at the deadline, after terminating *Assess and fix*. In this case, the event subprocess end event *Rescheduled* represents a second end state, in addition to the normal child-level end state, which we have labeled *Fix complete*. Following Method and Style, we now need a gateway to test which end state did the instance reach, as seen in the top-level diagram.

CHAPTER 8

Instance Alignment

We're almost at the end. I've been putting off this issue, but now we need to face it. This is BPMN's nasty requirement that the instance of each activity in a process must correspond to an instance of the process. If the process instance is an order, every activity in it must be performed once an order, not once a day or once a batch of orders. But batching is commonplace in real-world processes, so we need to deal with it. In this chapter we'll see various ways to do it: loop and multi-instance activities, multi-process structures, and non-interrupting Message event subprocesses.

Loop Activity

A *loop activity*, indicated by a circular arrow marker at bottom center (Figure 8-1, left), is like Do-While construct in programming. It means the same thing as the explicit gateway-loopback diagram on the right: perform the activity once, and then evaluate the *exit condition*, denoted by the text annotation *Loop until x*. Based on this test, either exit or perform the activity a second time and evaluate the loop condition again, and so forth until the exit condition is met.

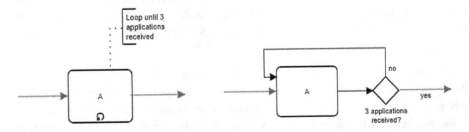

Figure 8-1. Loop activity A (left) means the same as non-loop activity A with gateway-loopback

A loop activity may be either a task or a subprocess. Don't use the loop marker and gateway-loopback together. That's a loop within a loop, probably not what you mean. With loop activities, the iteration is always sequential. You can't start the second iteration until you have finished the first, so looping is practical only when the cycle time for a single iteration is relatively short. Also, with a loop activity, the *number of iterations is unknown* when the first iteration starts. It is determined by evaluating the loop condition at the end of each iteration.

Multi-Instance Activity

A *multi-instance (MI) activity*, denoted by a marker of 3 parallel bars at the bottom center, is like For-Each in programming. It means perform the activity once for each item in a list. In a single process instance there are multiple instances of the activity, and each activity instance acts on one item in the list. What list? A multi-instance activity only makes sense when the process instance data contains some kind of collection, such as items in an order. In an order process, MI activity *Check stock* means check the stock of each order item.

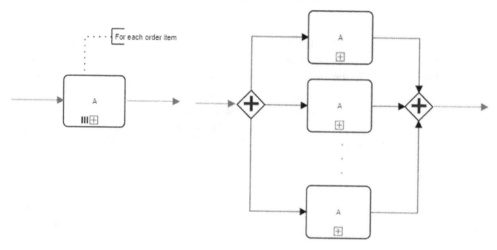

Figure 8-2. MI activity *A* (left) is the same as n parallel instances of non-MI activity *A* followed by a join (right).

Each order does not have the same number of items, but when *Check stock* begins for a particular order, you already know how many iterations will be required. It's the number of items in the order. Often the list involved is obvious from the activity name, but if not, best to indicate it in a text annotation, such as *For each X*.

Knowing the number of iterations in advance is one fundamental difference between multi-instance and loop activities. Another is that MI instances may be performed in parallel. If so, the MI marker is 3 vertical bars. If, on the other hand, the instances are always performed sequentially, the marker is 3 horizontal bars. A sequential MI activity is *not* the same as a loop. With MI you have a list; with loop you do not. It's best not to use an interrupting Error event on a multi-instance activity, since throwing the Error from any one instance will immediately abort all instances.

Instance Alignment with Repeating Activities

Figure 8-3 is a fragment of a hiring process. The instance is a job opening; every job opening goes through this process. But there is something terribly wrong with this diagram. See if you can tell what it is...

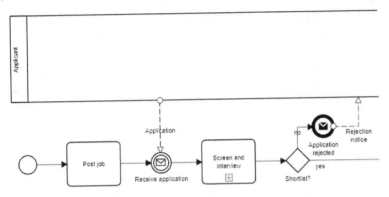

Figure 8-3. A common beginner mistake

This process *handles just a single application* for each job opening. Once the first one is received, the process instance has moved past *Receive application*, so there is nothing to catch another message. In reality, each job opening has to handle a batch of messages. *Receive application* should be once per application, while the process is once per job opening. It's that instance alignment issue again!

Repeating activities are the simplest way to deal with instance alignment issues, so let's see if that works here. We don't know how many messages we'll get, so we can try a loop.

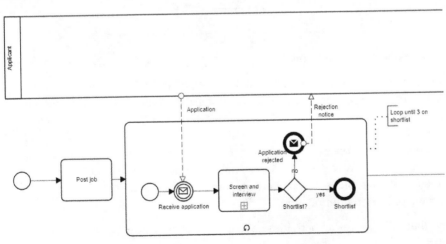

Figure 8-4. A valid but impractical solution

Let's wrap *Receive application* and *Screen and interview* in a subprocess and put a loop marker on it (Figure 8-4). Candidates passing the interview are put on the shortlist, and we loop until we have 3 on that list. This technically works, but it has a serious practical problem. The second iteration cannot begin until the first is complete. Arranging and completing the interview of Applicant 1 might take two or three weeks, and we cannot even look at Applicant 2 until that is complete, so this process is not going to work. If we are going to use a loop, it has to be relatively fast.

A more practical approach might be to have a fast *Receive and Screen* loop followed by an MI *Interview candidate* subprocess. *Receive and Screen* just sorts applicants into qualified candidates – those who match the basic qualifications – and non-qualified ones. This can be done very quickly by an HR assistant. Let's say the loop condition is *Loop until 5 qualified*. Then *Interview candidate* can be MI because we now have a list. We can conduct the interviews of all five candidates in parallel. When they are all done, we go on to *Make offer*. Now it looks like this:

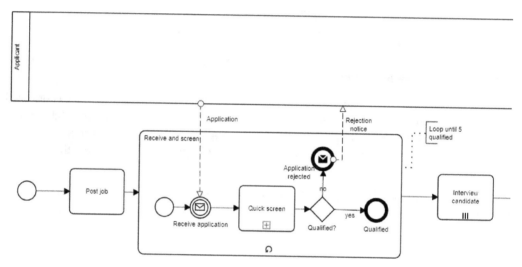

Figure 8-5. A more practical process model

This pattern using a fast loop activity to gather a list followed by an MI activity to process the list is straightforward, and if it works in your scenario it's a good one to use. But here it is still not quite right. The basic problem is that *Receive and Screen* and *Interview candidate* occur sequentially; they cannot overlap in time. We cannot start any interviews until we have all five viable candidates, and once we begin the interviews we cannot look at any more applicants. This may be the way your process actually works, but most people say, no, we'd like to begin interviews as soon as we have one qualified candidate, and keep looking at new applicants after we've started interviewing.

You cannot do that with repeating activities. We'll see a couple ways to do it, but they are more complicated.

Multi-Process Structures

It's always best to model an end-to-end business process as a single BPMN process if you can. But sometimes you cannot do that, and the reason is that activity instances are not aligned across the whole end-to-end process. There is no 1:1 correspondence between them. If repeating activities does not resolve the problem, you may need to model it using multiple BPMN processes. Our hiring process scenario provides a good example (Figure 8-6).

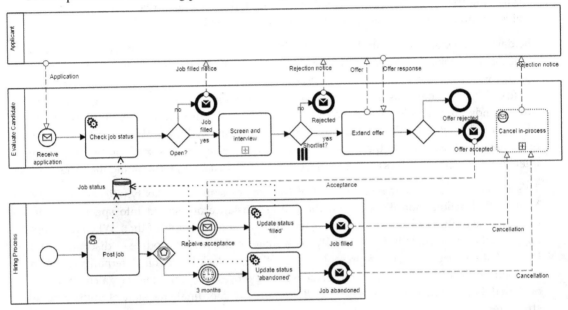

Figure 8-6. Multi-process solution to the hiring scenario

Now we have two processes: *Hiring Process*, in which the instance is a job opening, as before, and *Evaluate Candidate*, in which the instance is given by the start message, an application. These are separate processes not because different actors are performing them – they are the same in both processes. They are separate because the instances have 1:N correspondence, not 1:1. The 3-bar multi-participant marker[16] on *Evaluate Candidate* signifies there are N instances of this process running per 1 instance of *Hiring Process*.

This structure works because a top-level process like *Evaluate Candidate* has a freedom that a loop or MI activity does not. Recall that a Message start event has that magical ability to create a new process instance whenever the start message arrives. We don't need to know how many start messages will arrive. The Message start event creates a new instance for each one. And there is no rule that one instance must complete before the next one starts. The instances may overlap in time in any manner. This combines the best parts of loop and multi-instance activities, without their constraints.

---

[16] Displaying this marker is optional, even in Method and Style.

There are many possible solutions using this multi-process structure. In this one, *Hiring Process* just posts the job opening and waits to fill it. All the real work is done in *Evaluate Candidate*, which takes each application from receipt to final disposition. Now it doesn't matter how long that takes because processing one instance does not affect processing of other instances. They can overlap in any fashion.

This is perfect, but separate processes are independent, so we need to provide means of coordinating their activity. Remember that in BPMN, there are only two ways a process can receive information from outside: message and shared data. We'll use both here.

The data store *Job status* is central to the coordination. When we post the job, we create a row in the *Job status* table to say this particular job is open, and when we fill the job or abandon the posting, we update *Job status* to closed. As each application is received in *Evaluate Candidate*, the first thing that happens is checking that *Job status* table. If the job is no longer open the process ends immediately. When we fill the position, that will prevent new applicants from continuing *Evaluate Candidate*, but we also need to flush out candidates already in the midst of *Screen and Interview*. To do that, upon closing the job *Hiring Process* sends a message to an interrupting event subprocess in the top level of *Evaluate Candidate*, terminating the instances.

This perfectly matches our scenario, but at the cost of some complexity. Recall from the Method that actions not aligned with the process instance are sorted into special buckets defining one or more additional processes, and this is a good example of that. When that non-aligned action is a single isolated activity, as we had in the weekly update of discount codes in the Method chapter, we can represent it abstractly as a black-box pool. Alternatively, when we want to show its details, we can represent it as a process pool. Either way, a combination of shared data and message flows is typically required to coordinate the state of multi-process structures.

Handling Batching in BPMN

The multi-process hiring solution may seem obscure, but for end-to-end process modeling you may find yourself using it frequently. A common use case is where one part of the process operates on "batches" of items that are processed one at a time in another part of the process. For example, in the order process examples used in this book, the process instance is a single order, meaning that end-to-end processing is one order at a time. But in real order processes, there may be a mainframe batch program that runs one or more times a day to post all orders received since the previous batch. It is not really correct to insert an activity *Post order batch* in the middle of a process where the instance is a single order, since that suggests *Post order batch* is repeated for each individual order.

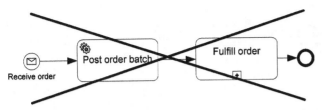

Figure 8-7. Instance mismatch between activity and process

Post order batch is better represented as an independent top-level process, with a Timer start event signifying a recurring process that interacts with the order process. As we saw with the hiring process example, there are two ways to model the interaction, shared data (Figure 8-8) and message flow (Figure 8-9).

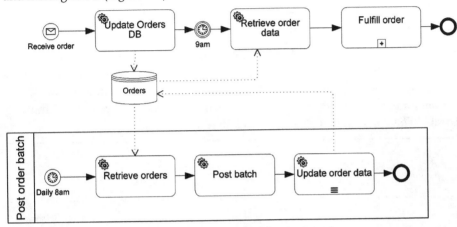

Figure 8-8. Two pools interacting via data store

In Figure 8-8, the *Order* process updates the *Orders* data store with each order as it is received. Once a day, the *Post order batch* process retrieves all the new orders, runs the batch, and updates the *Orders* database with the posting data. The *Order* process waits until the batch posting is scheduled to be complete, retrieves the posting data for that order, and continues.

In Figure 8-9, collection of daily orders is the same, but the posting info is returned to the *Order* process in a message. The process waits for the message, and continues as soon as the message arrives. With either the structure of Figure 8-8 or Figure 8-9, it is not necessary to show the process logic of *Post order batch* if your objective is modeling the *Order* process. You could model it as a black-box pool. The key thing is you cannot model the batch posting as an activity inside the *Order* process.

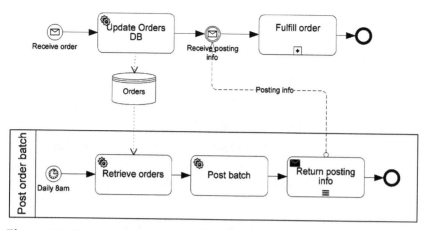

Figure 8-9. Two pools interacting via data store and message

The multi-process structure works in other cases besides batch programs. For example, in many of the examples in this book, an invoice is sent to the customer with each order. But for regular customers it is not uncommon to send a bill every month, not with every order. In that case, you cannot make *Send monthly statement* an activity in the *Order* process. It must be part of a separate *Billing* process that runs every month (Figure 8-10).

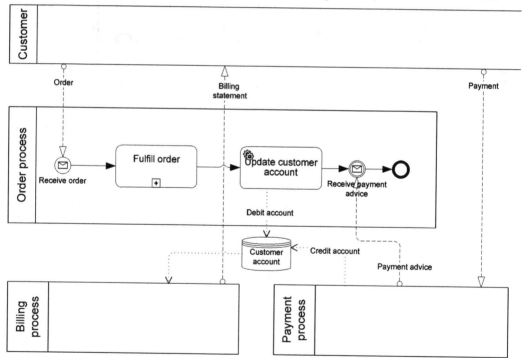

Figure 8-10. Billing and Payment are separate pools because the instance is not an order

Similarly, customer payments are not once per order or even necessarily once per month. An instance of the *Payments* process is once per payment. Thus if the *Order* process does not end until the order is paid for, multiple interacting pools are required.

Using Non-Interrupting Message Event Subprocesses

If you don't like the complexity of multi-process structures, there is a way to model many of these scenarios in a single BPMN process, although it, too, is a little complicated. A *non-interrupting Message event subprocess* possesses much of the freedom of a top-level process. An incoming message always triggers a new instance. You don't need to know how many there will be, and the instances may freely overlap in time. So in some ways, this pattern is simpler than the multi-process structure, but it has the additional complication that you cannot use message flows to coordinate state between the instances, just shared data and Terminate events.

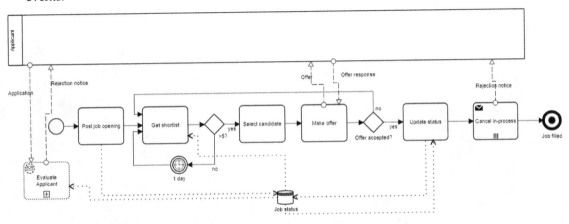

Figure 8-11. Hiring process using non-interrupting Message event subprocess

Figure 8-11 is a version of the hiring process scenario using a single process with a non-interrupting Message event subprocess. Now receiving, screening, and interviewing an applicant are inside *Evaluate Applicant*, the event subproces. We've moved the candidate selection and offer activities to the main process.

We still have the problem of coordinating state between the main process and the instances of *Evaluate applicant*. It's a little trickier now, because we cannot use messages, only shared data. So there is a lot of polling of data stores required. And to keep the diagram simple, the data store *Job status* now holds not only the overall status of each job opening but the details of each job opening, the applications received and the status of each applicant, for example, rejected or on short list. *Get short list* queries the data store daily until there are more than 5 on the short list. Then there is a meeting to select one candidate for the offer. We make the offer and get the response. If rejected we go back to the short list again. If accepted, we update the job status to closed and get all the in-process candidates, and send them rejections. To end all the instances of *Evaluate Applicant* we simply use Terminate.

Is this simpler or harder than the multi-process structure? You decide.

CHAPTER 9

Becoming Proficient

Well, we've covered all of it. You now understand how BPMN is like and unlike traditional flowcharting. You understand what Good BPMN means and the discipline required to create it. You understand the relationship between end states and gateways. You know about process levels and the value of hierarchical modeling. You've learned about joins, deadline-triggered actions, sending and receiving, and event subprocesses.

You've learned about the importance of the process instance and various techniques to achieve instance alignment. You've learned the Method, a systematic approach to taming the chaos of your stakeholder workshop notes and turning them into properly structured BPMN. You've learned the style rules, key to ensuring your intended meaning is clear to anyone from the printed diagrams alone. It's all there in a shade over 100 pages.

Good BPMN is a skill separate from being able to facilitate stakeholder workshops, analyze a process for waste or customer satisfaction, or manage a BPM project. It's a very basic thing: Given a set of facts about how a process – existing or imagined – works, translate that into a set of diagrams that communicates the process logic clearly and completely. That's all it is, translation from words into pictures, but with discipline and attention to detail. But it's a fundamental skill needed for anything you do in the process domain, whether that's simply documenting a process, engaging in process improvement or redesign, or creating business requirements for an IT project. The great thing about BPMN is it's a standard, with many good tools to choose from and many practitioners you can communicate with.

But for most people, becoming proficient at Good BPMN requires more than reading about it. It requires practice, testing your understanding, and working with real BPMN tools. I strongly urge you to do that.

bpmnPRO

One easy and inexpensive way to gain practice is bpmnPRO, a gamification-based e-learning app. I developed it to teach BPMN Method and Style to those who don't so much need to create BPMN themselves as to understand precisely the meaning of diagrams created by others in their team. bpmnPRO has no "lecture" and uses no BPMN tool. Modeled after Duolingo, an iOS language-learning app, it teaches the material entirely through quiz questions and puzzles. Like a game, you learn by making mistakes, doing it again, and gradually leveling up until you've covered everything.

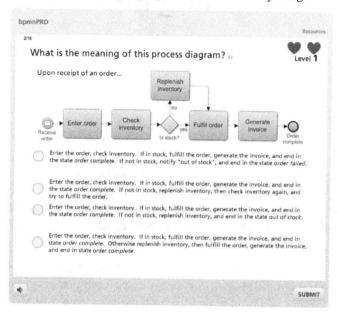

Figure 9-1. bpmnPRO focuses on matching text to BPMN diagrams

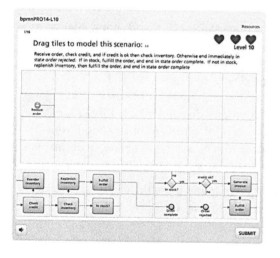 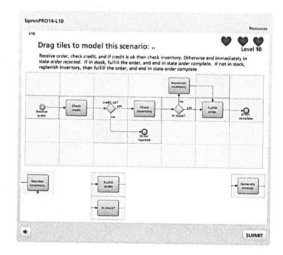

Figure 9-2. bpmnPRO uses puzzles to assemble diagrams matching the scenario

With bpmnPRO you progress through 10 levels. At the beginning, the focus on careful matching of the text to the diagram (Figure 9-1). At higher levels, the focus changes to the style rules, such as matching gateway and end state labels, and proper use of Message, Timer, and Error events. In lieu of a BPMN tool, some items involve arranging tiles to create a BPMN diagram matching a given scenario (Figure 9-2). When you make it all the way through bpmnPRO, you will be reasonably proficient at understanding Good BPMN.

bpmnPRO runs in any web browser. You can get it on my website methodandstyle.com.[17]

Training and Certification

Without a doubt, the best way to become proficient is BPMN Method and Style training and certification. That gives you hands-on practice with leading BPMN tools and forces you to master the parts of BPMN you're not so sure about. Any BPMN training will teach you the meaning of the shapes and symbols, but only Method and Style training adds the style rules and the systematic Method for reorganizing process information into Good BPMN.

The training is offered in a variety of formats: self-paced web/on-demand, live/online, and for your whole team, live at your company site. The content is the same for all three and very close to the content in this book. The difference comes from the in-class exercises and post-class certification.

In class, students create models following a given scenario, and we discuss the solution. This gives you a bit of practice, but at the end of the class most students are not yet proficient. Proficiency really starts with the post-class certification, which is based on two steps: an online exam and a mail-in exercise. It's in studying for the exam and completing the exercise that the classroom learning really sinks in. Once a student has passed the exam, he or she creates a process model that follows Method and Style and contains certain required elements, and sends it to me for review. If it's not perfect – and usually that is the case on the first attempt – I will point out the issues and ask the student to fix and resubmit. This cycle repeats until the exercise is perfect. Perfecting the certification exercise has proven to be the most effective way for students to become confident – and competent – process modelers.

BPMN Method and Style training is available through bpmessentials.com[18] and methodandstyle.com.[19]

---

[17] https://methodandstyle.com/bpmnpro/

[18] www.bpmessentials.com

[19] https://methodandstyle.com

Index

About the Author

Bruce Silver is founder and principal of BPMessentials, the leading provider of BPMN training and certification, as well as principal of methodandstyle.com, provider of BPMN and DMN training and certifications. He was a member of the task force that developed the BPMN 2.0 specification in OMG, and contributed to OMG's OCEB BPM certification exam. His book *BPMN Method and Style, 2nd Edition*, remains the standard reference on BPMN 2.0, and is available in English, German, Japanese, and Spanish.

In addition, he is a member of the Decision Model and Notation (DMN) task force and TCK, and author of *DMN Method and Style*, and founder/co-chair of bpmNEXT, an annual showcase of the next generation of BPM technology. His website methodandstyle.com provides news, commentary, and resources for practitioners of business process and decision modeling, and his company Bruce Silver Associates provides training and consulting in those disciplines.

Prior to founding Bruce Silver Associates in 1994, he was Vice President in charge of workflow and document management at the analyst firm BIS Strategic Decisions, which became Giga (now part of Forrester Research). He has Bachelor and PhD degrees in Physics from Princeton and MIT, and four US Patents in electronic imaging.

To contact the author, email bruce@brsilver.com.

CPSIA information can be obtained
at www.ICGtesting.com
Printed in the USA
FSHW021345040121
77397FS

9 780982 368169